# EMOTIONAL FREEDOM

## THE CHOICES WE MUST MAKE

Jane Ault

WESTBOW PRESS
A DIVISION OF THOMAS NELSON
& ZONDERVAN

Copyright © 2015 Jane Ault.

All rights reserved. No part of this book may be used or reproduced by any means, graphic, electronic, or mechanical, including photocopying, recording, taping or by any information storage retrieval system without the written permission of the author except in the case of brief quotations embodied in critical articles and reviews.

The Scripture quotation used in Image 1 (in the Appendix of this book) is from the Holy Bible, English Standard Version® (ESV®), copyright © 2001 by Crossway, a publishing ministry of Good News Publishers. Used by permission. All rights reserved.

Scripture quotations marked NLT are from the *Holy Bible*, New Living Translation, copyright © 1996, 2004, 2007 by Tyndale House Foundation. Used by permission of Tyndale House Publishers, Inc., Carol Stream, Illinois 60188. All rights reserved.

Scripture quotations marked NIV are from the THE HOLY BIBLE, NEW INTERNATIONAL VERSION®, NIV Copyright © 1973, 1978, 1984, 2011 by Biblica, Inc.® Used by permission. All rights reserved worldwide.

Scripture quotations marked MSG are from *The Message*. Copyright © 1993, 1994, 1995, 1996, 2000, 2001, 2002. Used by permission of NavPress Publishing Group.

Scripture quotations marked NKJV are from the NEW KING JAMES VERSION®. Copyright © 1982 by Thomas Nelson. Used by permission. All rights reserved.

Scripture quotations marked NASB are from the NEW AMERICAN STANDARD BIBLE®, Copyright © 1960, 1962, 1963, 1968, 1971, 1972, 1973, 1975, 1977, 1995 by The Lockman Foundation. Used by permission.

Scripture quotations marked NCV are from the New Century Version®. Copyright © 2005 by Thomas Nelson. Used by permission. All rights reserved.

WestBow Press books may be ordered through booksellers or by contacting:

WestBow Press
A Division of Thomas Nelson & Zondervan
1663 Liberty Drive
Bloomington, IN 47403
www.westbowpress.com
1 (866) 928-1240

Because of the dynamic nature of the Internet, any web addresses or links contained in this book may have changed since publication and may no longer be valid. The views expressed in this work are solely those of the author and do not necessarily reflect the views of the publisher, and the publisher hereby disclaims any responsibility for them.

Any people depicted in stock imagery provided by Thinkstock are models, and such images are being used for illustrative purposes only. Certain stock imagery © Thinkstock.

ISBN: 978-1-5127-0836-3 (sc)
ISBN: 978-1-5127-0837-0 (hc)
ISBN: 978-1-5127-0835-6 (e)

Library of Congress Control Number: 2015913184

Print information available on the last page.

WestBow Press rev. date: 09/17/2015

*To*
Linda Cataldo Gerlach (1955-2004)
Kay Linda Popiel (1943- 2011)
Alice Joy Pike (1934-2014)
*Their prayers and words of encouragement
Continue to cheer me on*

# Acknowledgements

In my efforts to write this book, I've received an abundance of support. I am thankful for everyone who has cared about what I'm doing, encouraged me, and prayed for me. The people I've named have provided significant help.

Linda Gerlach, Kay Popiel, and Alice Pike—to whom I dedicated this book—were enthusiastic and faithful cheerleaders. Linda saw what God was doing in my life, joyfully confirmed it, and gave me opportunities to share my story. Kay looked forward to the completion of my manuscript with childlike delight, prayed for me, and called me daily during the last few months of her life to ask how it was coming. Alice believed that I had something special, told me so, and prayed for me continually—even while she battled cancer.

Irene Theobald had confidence that I could write, listened to my concerns, prayed specifically for them, and invited me to share the content of this book with members of her home-group: Debbie, Caroline, Donna, Steph, Yvonne, Jill, Amy, Judy, Penny G., Penny J., and Marvenia. They listened attentively to my weekly lessons, completed their homework, and provided me with "grace-filled accountability."

Crystal, Jody, Char, Heidi, Peppy, and Danny—members of my Sunday school class—arrived early on cold winter mornings, participated with eagerness, and gave me helpful feedback on the material in this book.

Stephanie Hebel, Donna Exware, Crystal Holt, Amy Crawford, Rose Peterson, Barry Scholz, and Judy Scholz permitted me to include their stories of faith and integrity.

Stephanie, my primary editor, checked my numerous revisions with promptness, accuracy, patience, and enthusiasm. Jack Oliphant prayed for me, encouraged me with his editorial insights and comments, and affirmed me as a writer. Carrie Marks, my daughter, took time from her busy teaching schedule to examine parts of my manuscript, give me her professional opinion, and help me find tools to understand grammar. Corinne Kelly Avery, my artist, connected with my vision, saw exactly what I wanted, and created an image (depicting the theme of this book) that took my breath away.

Dr. Peter Ladd, professor at St. Lawrence University, saw my passion to write long before I did, and he generously granted me permission to use his illustrative "maps" of emotional addiction in this book. As I studied and prayed over his maps, God showed me my need of emotional freedom.

John, my husband, cheerfully (and numerous times) made his own meals, cleaned up afterwards, kept our house reasonably clean, prayed for me, listened to me when I became discouraged, read my many revisions, researched and answered my "Does this reflect the accuracy of the Biblical text?" questions, and always gladdened me with a hug.

Jean, my beloved twin-sister, prayed faithfully, encouraged me with her comments, and always inspired me with her faith. Marty, my brother, validated my memories, shared some of his, and made spending time with me a priority.

Finally, and foremost of all Jesus Christ, my Lord and Savior, paid my emotional and spiritual debt, provided me with the opportunities that I needed to learn and grow, motivated me to make difficult choices, blessed me with the power to persevere, and comforted me with his presence.

# Preface

I am unashamedly a follower of Jesus Christ, and I deeply desire to live worthy of his love. I want to honor him by displaying his character qualities—love, joy, peace, patience, kindness, goodness, faithfulness, gentleness, and self-control—in my life. Although I've been growing in those qualities for approximately sixty-five years, I am admittedly still imperfect. Does that discourage me? Not really. I am following in the footsteps of notable saints of the past.

Paul, that giant first-century apostle of Jesus Christ and writer of most of the New Testament books, admitted as he neared the end of his life that he had not reached perfection. These are his words: "I don't mean to say . . . that I have already reached perfection. But I press on to possess that perfection for which Christ Jesus first possessed me" (Philippians 3:12 New Living Translation).

Like Paul, my goal is perfection, but I'm neither defining nor pursing perfection in the way that it's often defined; that is, faultless behavior produced *by me* through disciplined self-effort. The perfection that Paul was speaking of, and that I'm running after, is character transformation created *in me* by Jesus Christ through a bond of faith and love.

This character transformation necessitates my cooperation—which may be the primary reason for its slow development in my life. Understanding the process is also essential. I've been examining that process for many years. When I turned over the management of my life to Jesus, I expected that I would be instantly and miraculously transformed. Believing what my Christian mentors told me—that I was a new creation, I felt confident that I would be able to handle most of the required changes without God's help—and I assumed that very few would be needed.

That "faultless behavior produced *by me* through disciplined self-effort" approach did not work very well or very long for me; over the years as I've observed the struggles that other Christians have in regard to integrity, I've noticed that self-effort (living up to God's laws) doesn't produce faultless behavior for anyone. Its two outcomes are legalism and hypocrisy. The power for transformation comes through grace. Unfortunately, it's possible to say (and think) that we are living by grace, while in reality we are practicing law. That was true for me in the early years of my Christian life.

My wake-up call came in the form of depression, and I discovered that there is an unmistakable connection between emotional health and spiritual health. This is because the roots of our emotional life, like those of our spiritual life, reside in the unconscious realm of our personality called the "heart." Our emotions influence our spirits and our spirits influence our emotions. I'm convinced that we can't develop spiritual maturity without emotional integrity.

In order for us to develop emotional integrity, we need to (1) be aware of our emotions, (2) own our emotions (that is, stop blaming others for our anger and resentment), and (3) admit to our unhealthy emotional patterns. The ability to recognize emotions is an aptitude which varies with individuals but can be developed to the level needed for emotional health by anyone who is willing to work at it.

When we are afraid or ashamed of our emotions such as anger and resentment, we tend to hide them—from both ourselves and others. Influenced by the example and teachings of my family of origin and the Christian culture of which I was a part, I hid these and other scary and unacceptable emotions for many years. This habit eventually proved disastrous to my emotional and spiritual health.

I ended up in bondage to the emotions that I had hidden. Realizing that I, alone, was responsible for my condition yet powerless to change, I wrote the following lines in a poem:

> Entrapped by myself, I choose so to be,
> But freed from myself—no way can I see.
>
> By choices I made and followed each day,
> Impressions were made in my vessel of clay.
>
> Clay hardens in time and cannot be bent;
> Habits of mine are now shackles of cement.
>
> To alter my course, become a new form,
> Requires strength beyond my norm . . .

I did not have the power to release myself from the prison in which I'd placed myself; however, I was in deep pain and desperate for help. I searched and prayed for it. God heard my prayers and answered them. His help did not come in the form that I expected it would—immediate deliverance, but it was in the form that I needed it to be—a journey in which he gave me knowledge, understanding, and wisdom.

I wrote *Emotional Freedom: The Choices We Must Make* with the purposes of (1) testifying of God's goodness to me and (2) sharing the knowledge, understanding, and wisdom that he's given me with others who are eager to grow toward emotional and spiritual maturity.

If that's your desire, then I hope you will join me in this never-ending journey with Jesus Christ. As we remain with him, we are progressively set free.

# Contents

**PART ONE: DAMAGE in the Orchard**

**1. Oaks of Righteousness**................................................................1
God's promised destiny: "Solid-oak" emotional and spiritual integrity

**2. Aborted and Diseased "Fruit"**....................................................9
Our present reality: Immaturity and imperfection

**PART TWO: Groundwork for RESTORATION**

**3. The "Tree" Model of Emotion**...................................................17
Components of emotion: Roots, limbs and branches, leaves, and fruit

**4. Disconnection from the "Well"**..................................................27
Consequences of rejecting God: Emotional and spiritual emptiness

**5. Bonded to a Diseased Root**.......................................................33
Characteristics of the sin nature: Deception and powerlessness

**6. Transplanted into Healthy Soil**..................................................39
The Life-saving Transfer: God's love

**7. A Dynamic Dance with the Gardener**......................................45
The liberating rhythm: Grace and responsibility

**8. Nutrients for Growth**..................................................................53
Disciplines: Bible study, obedience, prayer-journaling,
worship, rest, and accountability

## PART THREE: Attain FREEDOM—
## Make the Necessary Choices

**9. Identify Dysfunctional Anger** ............................................. 69
Recognize the destructiveness of denial

**10. Choose Self-control and Become Productive** ................. 79
Learn constructive problem-solving

**11. Uncover Bitter Resentment** .............................................. 89
Expose camouflage styles of expression

**12. Embrace Truth and Discover Joy** ................................... 100
Make gratitude a lifestyle

**13. Admit to Stubborn Revenge** ........................................... 112
Acknowledge the chain of self-torture

**14. Prefer Mercy and Obtain Freedom** ............................... 123
Forgive, bless, seek reconciliation, and be healed

**STUDY GUIDE** ...................................................................... 139

**Appendix** ............................................................................... 179
**Notes** ..................................................................................... 189
**About the Author** ................................................................ 193

# PART ONE

# DAMAGE in the Orchard

# 1

## Oaks of Righteousness

Thirty-one years ago, while I sat on a sandy lakeshore in northern Michigan, God planted the seed for this book in my heart—although I didn't recognize it at the time. I was viewing the destructive effects of a thunderstorm. A giant oak that I loved had crashed. It seemed senseless. Wiping away a few tears, I walked over to the tree and examined it so that I could find out why it fell. Though its exterior bark was thick and strong, the inside had rotted away—so much so that it was practically hollow. Reflecting on this, I wrote the following lines in a poem.

> **Summer 1983**
> Lord, I've wanted to be like an oak,
> Confident and strong;
> But the shell that protected me
> Has left me hollow—alone.
>
> My soul left bare to the elements of fear,
> Disappointment, and pain,
> Can only be shaped to maturity
> As I rest in the strength of your arms.
>
> Lord, I remove my self-protective shell
> And extend my arms to you . . .

*Jane Ault*

I was like that beautiful but hollow oak. On the outside, I looked strong. I had a college degree, successful work experiences, a kind and loving husband, and two beautiful daughters. On the inside, I had deep inner pain and a gnawing sense of failure. I was deeply depressed and about to crash. Like that oak, I was diseased—full of shame, guilt, fear, and other destructive emotions.

Few people knew about my inner struggle, and I had little understanding about the cause. But, God knew about all of it. With grace and patience, he showed me the inner conflicts that fueled my depression and taught me how to find inward harmony and strength. I've received healing, and I've matured; yet I'm far from perfect.

Reaching emotional and spiritual maturity—health and freedom—is a lifelong journey. This maturity is not about perfection (as we normally define perfection). It's about *integrity*. Integrity involves having an undivided heart— being single-minded so that I don't shift from one position to another. It means giving myself wholeheartedly to something (or someone), dedicating my entire self to that task, or committing my entire life to that person. It's saying "yes" with my heart as well as my mouth.

## Integrity

Integrity is about keeping promises. More than that it's about my reasons for keeping promises and what kind of promises I keep. Keeping a promise can be self-serving. Emotional integrity—being truthful about my feelings can destroy others when criticism becomes unkind. Telling someone "I hate you" is unnecessary, even if I feel that way. Along with emotional integrity, I need moral integrity. Moral integrity is about discernment. It means choosing the pathway of love—making decisions based on love rather than convenience and sticking to them even when it costs us something. Amy, Barry, and Judy have chosen to walk the pathway of integrity and love.

Amy is caring for an invalid husband. Not long after they were married, her husband was in an accident and suffered crippling brain damage. She could have placed him in a nursing home, but in persistent love and faith, she continues to care for him herself. Talking about the difficult reality of her decision, she writes,

> I hate alone time sometimes because then I think too much. Not always, but sometimes alone time makes me think about all that is lost. It is compounded with a ticking clock because it's so quiet! I lean on God and feel His peace and joy most of the time. But there are moments [when] memories of life before Tom fell creep in. I find myself wishing I had a time machine to go back and change that day! This is the part of life where we are supposed to do everything we dreamed of and now he can't. Yet! I still believe in miracles and anything is possible!

Barry and Judy have a son with Down's syndrome. They've been able to see beyond his disabilities and recognize the beauty and sensitivity of Jason's spirit. For thirty-three years, they've advocated for him in order to provide for his educational, social, and health needs. I doubt if anyone understands what the cost of this commitment has meant for them; social isolation and rejection has been a huge one. "The journey would forever change the way we lived our life," said Judy. "We were unaware of the complex and overwhelming medical issues we would encounter. It's been hard, but I'm not bitter."

Neither Amy nor Barry and Judy pretend their lives have been easy. They are real. They possess emotional as well as moral integrity. Emotional integrity is foundational to moral integrity. We can't follow through on a moral promise if we lack emotional integrity—that is, if we are dishonest about our feelings. To become honest about our feelings we must be aware of them. It's all too easy to block out uncomfortable feelings. First we do it consciously, and then it becomes an unconscious habit.

When we ignore or are unaware of the desires and feelings of our heart we can end up saying "yes" with our mouths but "no" with our hearts. This prevents us from following through with our moral commitments. We become like the people of Israel, described in the Old Testament. They said to God, "Yes, we will keep the commandments." Yet, because of the conflicting emotions and desires of their hearts, they did not. They said one thing and did another.

Integrity is not so much about the choices we make as it is about the person we are. If we have integrity, we will keep small commitments as well as larger ones. For example, I promised the members of a class I'm teaching on Sunday mornings that I would make a Crockpot of steel-cut oatmeal for them. They liked the oatmeal so much that I told them I would make more the following week. When the following Saturday night arrived, I felt tired and did not want to bother with making the oatmeal. So, was it necessary to keep my promise?

My class members would have probably forgiven me if I hadn't kept it. However, since I teach and write on the topic of integrity, I really did not want to be a hypocrite and break my promise. Aside from that, it gave me satisfaction to know my students were eating a nutritious breakfast.

## Hypocrisy

*Hypocrisy*, the opposite of integrity, is pretending to be something we are not. It's the default mode for most of us. Why does hypocrisy seem easier than integrity? Sometimes it's related to our need for connection, our sense of self-worth, and our confusion about identity.

If we have a clear sense of identity and a strong sense of self-worth, we can afford to face rejection. But if we feel insecure and our sense of self-worth is based on what others think of us— if we're getting our value in life from the opinions of other people—then we can't afford to risk offending them by disagreeing with their point of view. It's safer to hide our thoughts, put on a happy face, and feel depressed. Hiding feels safer, but it's destructive. We lose touch with reality and become confused about our identity.

We might fall into hypocrisy because we don't think through the cost of a commitment before making it. When that happens we may regret making the promise and not fulfill it or fulfill it grudgingly. We might give hypocritical double-messages to people because we are unaware of what our hearts desire.

We might *prefer* ignorance because we don't think it's important to know the condition of our hearts; we may be fearful of what we might find there or too lazy to go through the hard work of finding out. Discovering that we have a diseased heart is painful. Picturing myself as a diseased oak shocked me. Examining the roots of the disease and making changes was very hard work. It's only by the grace of God that I have been able to do those things, but I have no regrets.

Although I still fall into my old patterns of emotional dysfunction, I'm no longer enslaved by them. More of the time, I'm the same on the outside as I am on the inside. I no longer hide behind a self-protective armor—pretending to be strong when I feel weak, denying anger when I'm inwardly seething, covering resentment with a smile, and mouthing forgiveness when I'm planning revenge.

Because God empowers me, I've made significant changes—more often, I admit to weakness; more quickly, I acknowledge anger (and express it in constructive ways); more frequently, I feel grateful; more easily, I let go of grudges; and more thoroughly, I forgive.

It feels tremendously satisfying to have this kind of integrity. Although, it's not something I achieved by self-effort—it did (and does) involve work. The work is a work of faith. I believe the truths of Scripture and apply them in everyday situations according to the direction I receive from Jesus. Through the power of the Holy Spirit, my inner life continues to be transformed. I'm becoming an "Oak of Righteousness."

## A Promise of Healing

"Oaks of Righteousness" is the phrase the Old Testament prophet Isaiah used to describe broken-hearted people whom God was healing and setting free. This is his message:

> The Spirit of the Sovereign Lord is on me . . .
> He has sent me to bind up the brokenhearted,
>   to proclaim freedom for the captives . . .
>   to comfort all who mourn,
>   and provide for those who grieve in Zion—
> to bestow on them a crown of beauty
>   instead of ashes, the oil of joy
>   instead of mourning, and a garment of praise
>   instead of a spirit of despair.
> They will be called oaks of righteousness,
>   a planting of the Lord
>   for the display of his splendor.
>     —Isaiah 61:1–3 (New International Version)

"Oak of Righteousness" is my new (and true) identity. It's the identity of all followers of Jesus Christ who are undergoing Holy Spirit-empowered character transformation. In celebration of that truth, I recently wrote the following lines of a song.

## Winter 2014

> We are oaks of righteousness,
> Oaks of righteousness—
> Planted by the Lord.
>
> Let's rejoice in our destiny,
> Become what we're designed to be—
> Embrace the Creator of our souls.

Embracing Jesus Christ transforms us into people who have solid-oak integrity. He sets us free from the destructive and addictive emotions which eat away our inner self—causing us to feel ashamed and put on a false Christian front. Through the knowledge, understanding, and acceptance of truth—and the empowerment of God's Spirit, we can learn how to express anger in a self-controlled manner, turn from bitterness to joy, and choose to forgive and bless others instead of pursue revenge. That is what this book is about.

For the past year, I've been teaching these concepts to a small group of women, as well as a Sunday school class. My students have experienced significant emotional and spiritual growth. Donna graciously gave me permission to share what she's experienced. These are her words:

> The lessons in Jane's book have opened my mind and my heart to Jesus. With God's help, we can change the way we feel and think and act, so that we can bear good fruit. Now, I can see myself the way God sees me: caring, loving, happy, and strong—eager to learn and bring the word of Jesus to others. I have learned that to forgive others brings as much peace to me as it does to the person I've forgiven. By believing in Jesus, we are all the children of God. He loves us all and forgives our sins if we ask him to. I feel comfortable,

now, just talking to Jesus any time of the day. As I go about my day, I praise him or worship him in song. Jesus is like a close friend who can be trusted with your feelings, and he is always there. Before Jane's lessons I saw parts of my life as a disaster. Now I see them as a blessing, part of God's plan for me.

I've inserted more of Donna's story, comments from other class members, and many of my own personal examples in the following chapters. I've included these illustrations to show you that the concepts in my book work and to help you understand how to apply them.

I hope you will turn your attention to God and discover how amazing, powerful, patient, loving, and faithful *he is*. Then you will become the beautiful person of integrity he meant for you to be.

# 2

# Aborted and Diseased "Fruit"

> I decide to do good, but I don't really do it; I decide not to do bad, but then I do it anyway. My decisions, such as they are, don't result in actions. Something has gone wrong deep within me and gets the better of me every time.
> —Romans 7:19–20 (*The Message*)

Each week, my husband teaches a class at our local rehab center. Often the addicts he speaks to are third or fourth-time repeaters. They've decided to stop using drugs and alcohol. They've received help. They've hoped and expected to stay sober, yet they've not followed through with their good intentions—they've returned to their former habits. The man my husband visited today said, "I've been through rehab five times." He might identify with the statement—"Something has gone wrong deep inside of me and gets the better of me every time."

Though I've never been drunk, never smoked marijuana, never snorted cocaine, and never injected heroin into my veins, I have no basis for looking down at people addicted to these substances. Too often I fail to follow through with the good that I desire and intend to do. More often than I like to admit, I find myself doing the bad that I don't want to do.

Every day, every week, every month, and every year, I begin with hopes and expectations that I will do better than I did yesterday. I will make that phone call, write that letter, visit that friend, control my quick temper, spend less time on Facebook, more time at my piano worshipping God, and gracefully accept defeat in a Scrabble game. Some days I succeed. Some days I do not. I don't think my failures are evident to most people.

On the outside, I look like a perfect Christian. I attend church regularly. On several occasions, I've preached sermons and taught at retreats. Occasionally, I sing in the Christmas choir or lead worship for the people who meet in my small home group. I'm thankful for and careful with material blessings. I support missionaries. I care for the needs of my husband, children, and grandchildren. I'm a responsible citizen. I vote and obey the speed limit—most of the time. Still, too often I fail to recognize the *hidden* emotions that sabotage my will. As a result, I abort my plans for doing good and give in to behaviors I want to avoid.

Consider the following examples:

- I decide to visit the woman who has recently moved next door and welcome her into the neighborhood. Recalling the hassle of moving, I want to make life a bit easier for her. I think about preparing a meal, but I hesitate—maybe she won't like what I fix. I tell myself that I have enough to do. Weeks go by. Weeks lengthen into months. Eventually, I feel too embarrassed to make a call, so I simply avoid my neighbor. Could staying busy and playing computer games be ways that I block out my feelings of discomfort?
- I send a valuable gift to a close relative, but there is no acknowledgment of my present. I don't know why she fails to respond. Instead of trying to find out, I close my heart to her and withdraw, telling myself that I don't need that relationship; I can get along without family. I decide that

if she wants a relationship with me, then she'll have to take initiative, but I may or may not respond. I blame her for the loss of relationship. Not remembering the occasions that I neglected to write a thank you note, I fail to recognize my resentment.

- Determining not to exceed my budget when I grocery shop this month, I list the items I actually need and tell myself I will buy only those items. When I arrive at the store, I pick up the sale flyer and browse through it; then, ignoring my list, I fill my cart with bargains. As a result, I've exceeded my entire monthly budget, and the month is only half over. Justifying my expenditure and covering over my greed, I say to my husband, "You can now receive a fifty cent per gallon discount savings on gas!"

I can tell myself that these kinds of discrepancies are not all that important—God doesn't expect perfection. Why make a big deal about it? I start comparing my behavior with other people, particularly those who struggle with addictions, and I feel rather pleased with my performance. But that feeling of pleasure does not last long; I soon sense the Spirit of God is grieved by both my heart attitude and the lies I'm telling myself.

Putting on a false front makes me arrogant and leads me down the road of self-deception. Failing to recognize and admit to the self-centered and destructive thoughts in my heart makes me more vulnerable to acting them out. Unless I recognize and confess my spiritual poverty, I'll never receive the blessing of forgiving and empowering grace.

## Perfection Redefined

God sees beyond our external good behaviors. The real issue in life—the thing which counts in His eyes—is the condition of our hearts. The Old Testament prophet Samuel said to people of Israel who were looking for a king, "The Lord does not look at the things people look at. People look at the outward appearance, but the Lord looks at the heart" (1 Samuel 16:7 NIV).

Telling ourselves that God does not expect perfection is misleading because his concept of perfection is beyond ours and different from ours. When we think of perfection, we think of doing everything without error. God's concept of perfection is about *being* not just doing. The word which Jesus used when he told his disciples they were to be *perfect* like their Father in heaven (Matthew 5:48 NIV) comes from the Greek word *teleios*. Teleios means mature, and it refers to character change not simply outward behavior.[1]

Becoming perfect (mature) means becoming like Jesus—growing until we possess *his* perfection [*his* character traits]. (Ephesians 4:13 New Century Version). It means becoming "fully mature adults, fully developed within and without, fully alive like Christ" (Ephesians 4:13 MSG).

It means learning to love what Jesus loved (righteousness) and hate what he hated (wickedness). (Hebrews 1:9 NIV)

It means learning to honor our heavenly Father as Jesus did. People rejected him, but he did not care about his own honor. (John 8:49, 50 NIV)

It means learning to think like Jesus did. "Though he was God, he did not think of equality with God as something to cling to. Instead, he gave up his divine privileges; he took the humble position of a slave and was born as a human being . . . he humbled himself in obedience to God and died a criminal's death on a cross" (Philippians 2:6–8 NLT).

It means responding in every frustrating, difficult, and painful situation like Jesus did. He consistently displayed what the Bible calls fruit of righteousness: love, joy, peace, patience, kindness, goodness, faithfulness, gentleness, and self-control. (Galatians 5:22, 23 NIV)

In his humanity, Jesus was as vulnerable as we are, yet he did not buy into the destructive lies Satan tempted him with. He always responded with emotional and moral integrity. Not once did he react with inappropriate anger. Never did he accumulate resentment though grudge-bearing. In no way did he seek revenge. He had no reason for feeling guilty, was not the least bit greedy or egotistical, and did not—in envy—compare himself with anyone.

His intimate connection with God the Father sustained him in times of deep rejection by his own people. Although his disciples were slow to learn, he did not desert them; instead, he persevered with them to the end of his life. Even when facing the unimaginable stress of the cross, he did not allow anxiety or pain to determine his decision. What motivated him to persevere? He looked ahead and saw the joy obedience would bring him. (Hebrews 12:2 NLT)

I deeply want to possess this Jesus-kind of emotional maturity. I want to become the oak of righteousness he designed me to become. I know that living as he did would bring me unimaginable joy—the joy of intimacy with my Creator. I don't want to be a hypocrite. I want to have integrity—to be the same on the outside as I am on the inside—so that I can fulfill my commitments.

What makes it so hard for me to align my actions with my heart desires? And why do I continue to give in to desires that I detest? Perhaps my conflicts are not so different from those of the people in the rehab center with whom I'm tempted to favorably compare myself. What blocks us all from following through on our good intentions so that we can accomplish desirable and worthy goals?

A primary reason for this failure is that we don't understand the complexity of our emotions. The "Tree Model of Emotion" presented in the next chapter illustrates the relationship between our intentions and our behavior.

# PART TWO

## Groundwork for RESTORATION

# 3

# The "Tree" Model of Emotion

> A view of human nature that ignores the power of emotions is sadly shortsighted. For better or worse, intelligence can come to nothing when emotions hold sway.
>
> —Daniel Goldman[1]

I grew up believing that emotions had enormous power, so much power that they had to be kept under cover. As a consequence, I hid many emotions. The thought of exposing them terrified me. My family did not talk about their feelings, and I learned at an early age how to suppress mine—especially anger. That would be upsetting to my mother who had a heart condition and could not take the stress of dealing with conflict. In my child mind, I assumed that she would have a heart attack if I said or did anything to make her feel upset. Since I did not want to be guilty of killing my mother, hiding my anger seemed the wise and safe thing to do.

The Scandinavian community in which I grew up was much like the one described by Garrison Keillor in his novel *Lake Wobegon Days*. In the following vignette, he describes how difficult it is for the people in his fictitious hometown to talk about their emotions. The scene is the living room of a family whose members are gathered around their dying Grandmother:

*Jane Ault*

> We talked whispers, but didn't talk much; it was hard to know what to say. "Mother always said she wanted to go in her sleep," my mother said. "She didn't want to linger." I felt that we should be saying profound things about Grandma's life and what it had meant to us, but I didn't know how to say that I should. The women saw to Grandma and wept a little now and then, a few friendly tears; the men only sat and crossed and uncrossed their legs, slowly perishing of profound truth, until they began to whisper among themselves—I heard gas mileage mentioned, and a new combine—and then they resumed their normal voices. "I wouldn't drive a Fairland if you gave it to me for nothing," Uncle Frank said. "They are nothing but grief." At that time (twenty), I thought they were crude and heartless, but now that I know myself a little better, I can forgive them for wanting to get back onto familiar ground. . . [My grandmother] was eighty-two. Her life was in all of us in the room. Nobody needed to be told that, except me.[2]

One of my grandmothers died when I was in my twenties. After her funeral our family gathered in her home. Standing in the kitchen where Grandma had always prepared special foods for us—plates of warm, home-made biscuits topped with freshly-picked strawberries covered with real whipped cream, prune or peach-filled pastries which Grandma called kolaches, and sugar cookies so tender that they fell apart in our hands—standing in that place of happy memories, I couldn't hold back my tears. I fled to my grandmother's garden, threw myself down in the middle of it, and sobbed. Eventually, my mother found me. She looked at my red face and swollen eyes and scolded me, saying, "You mustn't cry; it will make your grandfather feel bad."

For years, I felt angry about her comment—until I understood that my mother's lack of tears did not mean she had an uncaring heart. The reason she scolded me was because I'd broken the following unspoken family rules: (1) You are responsible for the feelings of others. (2) It's wrong to cry when a loved one dies; you should rejoice because your loved one is in heaven.

We all have rules governing how we express emotions. Some of them are healthy, but some of them are not. When they are unspoken we don't recognize them as dysfunctional, so we keep on using them because in some weird way they make sense to us. Or even if they don't make sense, we continue using them because we don't know how to do things differently. Learning to identify our emotions and manage them in healthy ways is an essential skill. We differ in our ability to recognize our emotions, and we differ in our definition of *emotion*.

## What is Emotion?

Many people think emotion is a feeling inside of them—like anxiety—that comes and goes without any warning. These feelings float around us and within us like clouds in the sky, and we have no control over them. Other people think emotion is a behavior—like anger—that emerges with an outburst of dirty words or a slap in the face. These behaviors are scary and as unpredictable and dangerous as a tornado. We run from them.

For years I thought emotion was another word for feelings, and I did not think I could control my feelings very much. As I said, I was afraid of my own anger. I thought that if I did not block it, then it would get out of control—causing me to hurt myself and others. Hiding my anger did not make it go away. It contributed for many years to my depression and to the pain that I felt in my body.

Through a class that I took at St. Lawrence University, I learned that emotions develop in stages. I'm thankful for Dr. Peter Ladd's insights which gave me the knowledge I needed to begin making changes. My understanding and descriptive maps of emotion in this book and the subsequent ones are an adaptation of his concepts.[3]

## Emotion is Like a Tree

*For a helpful visual description of the following concepts, see the "Tree" Model of Emotion drawing (Image 1, page 179) in the Appendix.*

## Roots Represent Heart Beliefs

The roots of a tree are its foundation. We can't see most of them, but we know how important they are. When a tree is cut off from its roots, it falls over and dies. Trees with rotten, hollow roots (like the one I described in the beginning chapter of this book) crash quickly when storms descend on them. Trees with healthy roots withstand windy storms.

Like roots of a tree, our heart beliefs reside underground. They are beneath the level of conscious thought, yet it's important for us to identify them because they are the foundation of our emotions. With God's grace and help, we can uncover our heart beliefs and discover whether they are based on truth or on lies. King David realized that his heart contained "hidden sins" (Psalm 19:12 NLT) and asked God to reveal that which was "offensive" (Psalm 139:23, 24 NIV).

Root beliefs based on truth provide us with a foundation for emotional health. We will not crash under the stresses and storms of life.

Root beliefs based on lies supply a shaky foundation for emotional health. They give rise to unhealthy and destructive lifestyles which could become addictive. For example, if we believe in our hearts that we can't be happy without achieving the American dream of owning a house and having an income large enough to buy whatever we want, but our house is in foreclosure and we are unemployed, then our heart belief could make us vulnerable to emotions of envy, greed, and resentment.

## The Trunk, Limbs, and Branches Represent Conscious Thought

The trunk, limbs, and branches of a tree carry nutrients from the roots up through the branches and limbs. One of the joys that come with the arrival of spring in my county is sap time. By tapping sugar maples, syrup producers can discover when the sap starts to flow from the roots of the tree up to the branches. Collecting it and boiling it down is a time consuming process, but the sweet maple syrup that results is well worth it.

Just as sap flows from the roots of a tree up through its trunk, branches, and limbs delivering nutrition to the maple tree, so our heart beliefs flow into and give "life" to our conscious thoughts. These "above ground" thoughts are numerous. Keeping track of every thought we have would be time consuming and impossible, but it's important to pay attention to our major directions. If we want emotional health, then we must choose to think true, noble, right, pure, lovely and admirable thoughts. (Philippians 4:8 NIV)

Whether we express or hide them, our thoughts flow out of our heart beliefs. If we continually think about how we can get even with those who have hurt us, then we are in danger of becoming overcome by the desire for revenge. If our thought life flows with self-incriminating judgments, then we could become stuck in the emotion of guilt.

## Leaves Represent Feelings

The leaves of a tree swaying in the wind might not look like they are under the control of the tree's branches. However, they are attached to the branches and must move with them. Still, leaves covered with ice can affect the movement of the limbs, causing both limbs and branches to bend and break. As—within trees—roots, limbs, branches, leaves, and fruit are intimately connected and influence one another, so—within emotions—our heart beliefs, conscious thoughts, feelings, and behavior are intimately connected and influence one another.

Our feelings may seem to fluctuate with windy circumstances, but they are not caused by what happens around us. They are caused by what we *believe* about our circumstances and how we respond to them. Here's an example. If there's a storm during a winter night causing a loss of electric power, then several things will happen. The alarm clock will not go off, and I will oversleep. Without working appliances, I'll have no cup of coffee, and without hot water, I'll have no hot shower. Without the internet, I'll not be able to read my email. Because my heating system cannot operate without electricity, the temperature in my house will rapidly decline. What might I think, say, and feel?

I might say, "I feel angry because I can't take a hot shower, can't have hot coffee, and can't check my email." My anger is caused by what I *believe* about not having a hot shower, hot coffee, and the ability to read my email. If I believe that all of these things are essential and that I can't get along without them even for one hour of the day, I will feel deprived and angry, but if I *believe* I can be happy without these things, then there will be no need for me to feel anger. How I behave depends on what I think and feel. And how I feel is influenced by how I behave.

## Fruit Represents Behavior

The fruit of a tree is the tasty part—that which makes it desirable or undesirable. Most of us would not list lemons as our favorite fruit, although lemons that are picked right off the tree taste sweet to me. Just as fruit attracts or repels people based on the taste, so our behavior attracts or repels those around us. Most of us aren't attracted to sour-lemon behavior.

Behavior includes attitudes, actions, and words. Our behavior reflects and flows out of our feelings, thoughts, and heart beliefs. When we make a decision to withdraw or verbally attack someone, our actions are the outward expressions of our feelings. Verbal or physical abuse usually indicates the presence of anger. Withdrawing from a relationship could be the sign of resentment or apathy.

The quality of the fruit depends on the health of the tree. Just as it's impossible for a diseased apple tree to bear good apples, so it's impossible for an unhealthy emotion tree to produce healthy emotions. Jesus, who also used the tree as a parable, said that a healthy tree produces good fruit and a diseased tree produces "worm-eaten" fruit. (Matthew 12:33 MSG)

Healthy fruit (called "fruit of the Spirit") matches the attitudes and behavior of Jesus Christ. It develops out of our relationship with him. Unhealthy fruit (called "desires of the sin nature") matches the attitudes and behavior of the God-rejecting, ego-centered, Satanically-influenced constituents in the culture around us. It develops out of our dark side. In Galatians 5:19–23, Paul gives an excellent comparison of these two types of fruit. Other factors that affect the health of an emotion tree include its genetic make-up, the soil in which it grows, and the climate surrounding it.

## Tree Type Represents Genetic Predisposition

There are many types of fruit trees; each has a unique genetic makeup. They thrive under different conditions. My husband and I live in the northern part of the U.S. where lemons, oranges, and grapefruit trees do not survive. Apples trees, more hardy than citrus, do very well. One year we purchased an apple tree that had been genetically crossed with a Siberian apple tree. It thrived very well, and we picked apples from it in the same year that we planted it.

People of different nationalities and various genetic predispositions express emotion in distinct ways. For example, people of Scandinavian descent tend to be less expressive than those of Italian descent. Each of us is unique.

According to Dr. Elaine Aron, about 15-20 per cent of the U.S. population has highly sensitive nervous systems. She calls such people highly sensitive persons (HSP's). These people become overwhelmed when they are in a highly stimulating environment—bombarded by sights and sounds, for too long. Because they see, hear, and feel things with great intensity, they might be more vulnerable to anxiety than others.[4] Factors such as fatigue and illness, which alter our body chemicals, affect our emotional experience. Those of us with chronic pain could become addicted not only to pain killers but also to emotions such as anger, resentment, and apathy.

## Soil Represents Generational Patterns of Influence

The soil in which a tree grows affects its health. We planted our first Siberian apple tree in healthy soil. We were happy with its fruit, so when we moved to a new location, we planted a second similar tree in our front yard—unfortunately, in poor soil. The tree barely survived.

How generational patterns of thinking and behavior (the soil in which I grew) influenced my emotional behavior is illustrated by the following story. My grandmother owned a wood carving of three tiny monkeys. One of them had his hands over his eyes, one of them had his hands over his ears, and one of them had his hands over his mouth. "Look at these monkeys," Grandma said. "Listen to what they are saying. See no evil, hear no evil, and speak no evil!" That was my grandmother's motto. Her method for handling unacceptable emotions and emotional conflict was denial. There was no problem. I don't remember ever hearing her say, "I feel angry" or "I feel jealous." She half-way admitted to anxiety calling it "concern."

Will a "See no evil, hear no evil, speak no evil" slogan help us develop Christ-like character? It depends on what we mean by it. If using the slogan means that we recognize the destructive desires within us and are choosing to turn away from them, then it's helpful. But if using the slogan means that we are denying or covering up our destructive desires, then it hinders us from growing. That's the way I used it when I was growing up. I became an expert in the art of emotional denial.

Breaking out of emotional denial is painful. It's like becoming aware of a cancerous tumor. It will bring us tears. It will cost us something. We may need to spend our money and a lot of our time to receive the help we need to become emotionally healthy. We have to give up our pride—our insistence on looking good. I needed to do all of those things. It was painful. It was humbling. When I was ushered into the locked psychiatric ward of a hospital, I felt shocked and embarrassed. Now, years later, I feel extremely thankful to God because he allowed me to keep making unhealthy emotional choices until I got into such a condition of brokenness that I could no longer function. Then I was willing to receive the help he made available to me.

*Jane Ault*

## Climate Represents Social Environment: Family, Job, Local Community, and World

The climate a tree grows in affects its health and the quality of its fruit. We have several pine trees in our front yard that are dying. The branches are a sickly looking rust color. This is due to the effect of acid rain. Others trees are dying because of insects that have infested them.

The behaviors and feelings expressed within our family, community, and world systems affect our emotional experience. We tune in to verbal and nonverbal emotional messages and make adjustments depending on the depth of our need to be accepted. If I am a non-churchgoer and I work up the courage to visit a church, hoping to find friendship, but no one smiles and greets me or offers me a place to sit, then I will probably feel discouraged and not likely return.

The messages that we receive or do not receive from our social communities, such as Facebook, can powerfully impact our emotions and, consequently, our behavior. Shame and guilt messages are likely to pour out on us if we express an unpopular point of view or challenge the status quo. If we are insecure in our identity when this happens, then it's very difficult to retain our beliefs and not to react with destructive anger, resentment, or revenge.

Recognizing the complexity of our emotions can give us self-understanding, yet it doesn't explain what makes destructive desires so compelling that we give in to them and consequently abort our good desires. In order to acquire and maintain solid-oak emotional and moral integrity, we need to answer this question: why do destructive desires have such a grip on our souls?

# 4

## Disconnection from the "Well"

> My people have committed a compound sin: they've walked out on me, the fountain of fresh flowing waters, and then dug cisterns—cisterns that leak, cisterns that are no better than sieves.
> —Jeremiah 2:13 (MSG)

On the farm on which I grew up there were two storage containers for water—a cistern and a well. The cistern was a hole dug into the ground for collecting and containing rain water. During a drought the cistern might become empty, and sometimes it leaked. The well was a deeper hole. It was a more reliable source of water because it tapped into the underground water table. The cistern was covered with loose boards, and it contained rotted leaves and other debris. The well had a more protective covering, and on top of it there was hand pump.

I can remember seeing my father come in from the field on a hot summer day. His clothes were drenched with sweat, and his face was as red as my brother's wagon. He grabbed the handle of the well, pumped vigorously, and drank the cold water in long gulps. Then he paused and said, "There's nothing as thirst quenching as fresh, cold water!"

Being human, Jesus, too, experienced physical thirst. One day, after a long hike on a dusty road, he arrived at a well and sat down to rest. Soon, a woman came by; she was carrying a jug so that she could secure water from the well. Jesus asked her to give him a drink. She dipped the jug into the well, gave him a drink, and started talking to him. He offered her something called "*living* water." The conversation continued as follows:

> But sir, you don't have a rope or a bucket," she said, "and this well is very deep. Where would you get this living water? And besides, do you think you're greater than our ancestor Jacob, who gave us this well? How can you offer better water than he and his sons and his animals enjoyed?" Jesus replied, "Anyone who drinks this water will soon become thirsty again. But those who drink the water I give will never be thirsty again. It becomes a fresh, bubbling spring within them, giving them eternal life
> —John 4:11–14 (NLT)

## Spiritual Thirst

In his conversation with the woman, Jesus was talking about a spiritual thirst not a physical one. He knew this woman was spiritually thirsty because she'd been drinking polluted water out of a cistern that leaked. Since we are spiritual beings, not simply physical bodies, all of us experience spiritual thirst. That thirst is a need for a meaningful relationship with God—a relationship based on trust in which he fulfills our desires with his presence.

## A Trust Problem

When we desire to know God and we delight in him more than in anything else, Jesus satisfies our thirsty hearts—completely. But, for many of us, trusting and delighting in God has not been easy. In the beginning (in the Garden of Eden) it was different.

Adam and Eve trusted God. They walked and talked with him, and they listened to him. He gave them meaningful work and provided them with beautiful, safe, and comfortable surroundings. They enjoyed physical, mental, emotional, and spiritual well-being. Adam and Eve were happy and satisfied with life in the garden until Satan arrived (in the form of a serpent) and had a conversation with Eve. This is the story:

> Now the serpent was more crafty than any of the wild animals the Lord God had made. He said to the woman, "Did God really say, 'You must not eat from any tree in the garden'?"
> The woman said to the serpent, "We may eat fruit from the trees in the garden, but God did say, 'You must not eat fruit from the tree that is in the middle of the garden, and you must not touch it, or you will die.'"
> "You will not certainly die," the serpent said to the woman. "For God knows that when you eat from it your eyes will be opened, and you will be like God, knowing good and evil."
> —Genesis 3:1–5 (NIV)

Jesus called Satan a liar; he deceived Adam and Eve in the following ways:

- He aroused doubt in their minds—doubt about *their* ability to understand what God said and doubt about the *goodness* of

God's plan for them. I can imagine the sarcastic tone of voice Satan used when he asked that question: "Did God say?"
- He contradicted God, changing what God had told them: "You must not eat from the tree of the knowledge of good and evil, for when you eat from it you will certainly die" (Genesis 2:17 NIV) to "You will *not* certainly die" (Genesis 3:4 NIV). Satan changed God's words and he inferred that he was smarter than God. (He did this because he wanted Adam and Eve to trust him rather than God.) And, he implied that God was placing an unnecessary and mean restriction on Adam and Eve when he forbade them to eat of that one tree.
- He continued to raise doubts about God's character and goodness and made two more false promises saying, "For God knows that when you eat from it [the tree of the knowledge of good and evil] your eyes will be opened, and you will be like God, knowing good and evil" (Genesis 3:5 NIV).

Satan implied that God wanted to keep Adam and Eve ignorant. But they were not were *not* ignorant. God had given them great responsibility and clear instructions. Satan's "You will be like God" promise was extremely deceptive. Being created in God's image, Adam and Eve *were* like him—in character; but they were unlike him in authority. The choice that Satan tempted them with was to usurp God's authority (become their own God) and live independently of him. Satan did *not* tell them that doing so would make them unlike God—in character.

Adam and Eve chose to believe these lies about God, distrust him, and disregard his wisdom. Feeling dissatisfied with what he'd given them, they decided dependence on him was a hindrance, and they would rather be independent—make their own choices and fulfill their desires in the way they wanted to. God chose to respect their decision and evicted them from Garden.

## An Unwise Decision

Adam and Eve's decision to turn their backs on God—to divorce themselves from him—was the root of their problems. And it's the root of ours. It's what the Bible calls sin. Both Old and New Testament writers make it clear that we are no different from Adam and Eve. The prophet Isaiah compares us to straying sheep that have left God's paths to follow their own. (Isaiah 53:6 NLT) The Apostle Paul said, "Adam's sin brought death, so death spread to everyone, for everyone sinned" (Romans 5:12 NLT).

Although Adam and Eve did not instantly experience physical death, they lost the intimacy they had with God. Separated from him, they began to experience spiritual thirst. In the following quote, the prophet Jeremiah contrasts the painful thirst of those who depart from God with the blessedness of those who trust him:

> This is what the Lord says:
> "Cursed are those who put their trust in mere humans,
> > who rely on human strength
> > and turn their hearts away from the Lord.
> They are like stunted shrubs in the desert,
> > with no hope for the future.
> They will live in the barren wilderness,
> > in an uninhabited salty land.
> "But blessed are those who trust in the Lord
> > and have made the Lord their hope and confidence.
> They are like trees planted along a riverbank,
> > with roots that reach deep into the water.
> Such trees are not bothered by the heat
> > or worried by long months of drought.
> Their leaves stay green,
> > and they never stop producing fruit.
> > > —Jeremiah 17:5–8 (NLT)

Like Eve, I swallowed the lies that Satan told me. I believed that neither God nor my parents loved me. The truth was this: My parents loved the Lord, prayed for me, and took me to church from the time I was born. When we were four years old, my twin sister and I stood in front of the congregation at the church we attended and sang the words "Jesus loves me, this I know." While I consciously tried to believe what my parents and grandparents told me, in my heart I believed that Jesus loved only my sister—not me. And I did not trust him very much.

That was a root of the depression that I struggled with for many years. My heart felt like a parched desert. Unknown to my *conscious mind*, yet buried beneath my good behavior lay a cesspool of destructive desires and emotions—rage, resentment, revenge, envy, greed, anxiety, guilt and self-hatred.

I resisted becoming aware of these painful desires and emotions, but eventually God gave me the courage to become honest with myself. In his love for me, he continued uncovering lies and revealing truth to my thirsty heart. I have learned that I can trust him, and my love for him has grown deeper over the years.

Do I still struggle with destructive desires and emotions? Sometimes, but if I quickly recognize and reject them, they don't control my life to the extent that they used to. From time to time, all of us experience anger, anxiety, envy, guilt, jealousy, resentment, vengeance and greed. What happens if we deny the presence of such desires and emotions?

If we pretend long enough (lie to ourselves) that we don't have such feelings, then these destructive desires will disappear from our conscious mind. However, they will come to the surface at unexpected times and in unexpected ways. Our problem may be deeper and more complicated than we realize.

# 5

# Bonded to a Diseased Root

> There is a path before each person that seems right, but it ends in death.
> —Proverbs 16:25 (NLT)

During my high school years, I lived in a small town where everyone knew what everyone else was doing. Though I never entered the downtown tavern, I knew about the brawls that took place on Saturday night. Though I never tried it, I knew that some of my classmates sneaked out of class to smoke. Though I never tasted it, I knew about the hidden bottle of blackberry brandy that my grandmother kept for medicinal purposes.

## Emotional Addiction

*To help you understand the following concepts, please refer to the <u>Bonded to a Diseased Root</u> diagram <u>(Image 2, page 180)</u> in the Appendix.*

I didn't understand addiction but I knew it was not a good thing, and I felt rather smug about not being one of *those* people—the ones who got drunk and couldn't come to church on Sunday morning because they had a hangover. Many years went by before I learned that I, too, was addicted—not to substances but to desires and emotions. I expressed my pain in the lines of another poem.

> The world is full of many things that sound so good to me.
> Like the music of a carnival it cries, "Indulge yourself, break free!"
>
> I'm pulled in all directions, consumed by passion's fire,
> Content with nothing that I find—enslaved by my desire.
>
> Like cotton candy full of air is everything I buy;
> At first it tastes so sweet, but, soon, I find I'm dry—
>
> Unsatisfied, yet turning not to water that would fill my
> Parched and aching soul. Can there be pleasure in God's will?

The desires and emotions that controlled me and left me feeling so unsatisfied are what the Bible calls "works of the flesh." The use of the word "flesh" (in this context) does not refer to our physical bodies. It refers to the way we think, feel, and behave when we reject God and set ourselves up as gods. According to the Apostle Paul, these are the consequences:

> People did not think it was important to have a true knowledge of God. So God left them and allowed them to have their own worthless thinking and to do things they should not do. They are filled with every kind of sin, evil, selfishness, and hatred. They are full of jealousy, murder, fighting, lying, and thinking the worst about each other. They gossip and say evil things about each other. They hate God. They are rude and conceited and brag about themselves. They invent ways of doing evil. They do not obey their parents.

> They are foolish, they do not keep their promises, and they show no kindness or mercy to others.
> —Romans 1:28–31 (New Century Version)

In Galatians 5: 20 and 21, Paul places the following emotional conflicts in the category of works of the flesh: hostility, quarreling, jealousy, outbursts of anger, selfish ambition, dissension, division, and envy.

To describe these emotional conflicts, some Bible translations use the phrase *sin nature* (instead of the "works of the flesh" phrase); other translations use just the word *sin* instead of the *sin nature* phrase. I prefer using the term *sin nature* because I connect the word *flesh* with my body. My body is not evil. Also, sin nature refers to a characteristic. I think of it as a personality flaw not total personality. One of the characteristics of the sin nature is a predisposition to reject truth and believe lies.

## A Counterfeit Gold Ring

When we become a Christian we do not automatically get rid of the sin nature, and that nature does not weaken as we become older. Its urges become stronger. Like the deceitful and destructive pleading of the gold ring that Frodo (in *Lord of the Rings*) carried on a chain around his neck until the day he died, the sin nature remains with us for our entire life-journey.

Each of us posses a gold ring that's inscribed with lies. It's a worthless fake; but if we've adorned ourselves with it for years, then we will not easily give it up. Those lies seem sensible and right. "Wearing them" makes us feels comfortable and safe. We don't recognize that they are deadly. If we want to develop emotional and moral integrity—become oaks of righteousness—we must stop putting that ring on our finger. This means we must stop believing lies and begin to embrace truth. Developing this habit requires constant vigilance and many daily choices.

## Hope

Sometimes I get tired and discouraged with this long process; I feel like giving up. Then, in the middle of my struggle, God reminds me that he sees me as perfect. I don't understand how that's possible—although, I've heard lots of theological explanations. I do know that someday, either when Jesus comes again or I die, my struggles will be over; I will be like him. This is what the apostle John said:

> See how very much our Father loves us, for he calls us his children, and that is what we are! But the people who belong to this world don't recognize that we are God's children because they don't know him. Dear friends, we are already God's children, but he has not yet shown us what we will be like when Christ appears. But we do know that we will be like him, for we will see him as he really is. And all who have this eager expectation will keep themselves pure, just as he is pure.
> —1 John:3:1–3 (NLT)

What an incentive to reject lies and embrace truth!

As a child, I was very angry with God. I covered up my anger for so long that I was not aware of it until mid-life. Inwardly, I blamed him for hurts and rejections I'd received from others. At mealtime and in church, I bowed my head as an act of gratitude but my heart was arrogant and full of rage. I was enslaved to that sin nature. Like a chained handcuff attached to my will, it often pulled me away from the good that I (consciously) wanted to do and pushed me toward the bad that I (consciously) wanted to avoid. Yet, I did not believe I had a dark side.

## Our Dark Side

In his book, *The Heart's Desire*, James Houston writes: "If we do not adore God, with all our desire focused on him, we can only live enslaved like addicts to our senses . . . If we are not able to confront our own dark side—the capacity for evil within ourselves—we remain unaware of how destructive our addiction has become."[1]

In addition to a desire for him, God created us with desires for human relationships, meaningful work, material security, and emotional, mental and physical well-being. He created us with senses so that we could enjoy and appreciate the beautiful world he placed us in. He wants to fulfill all of these good desires. If we delight in him, he will give us the desires of our heart. (Psalm 37:4 New King James Version)

When we separate ourselves from God, denying or ignoring the spiritual thirst he's placed within us, we become prisoners to *all* of our desires—the good ones that God placed within us, as well as the destructive ones created by the sin-nature—and we are powerless to free ourselves. Consequently, we abort our good intentions and give in to our destructive desires. I illustrated this in chapter two with examples from my own life. The following (non-exclusive) list suggests additional ways that we abort good intentions and give in to destructive desires.

- We can't maintain healthy boundaries.
- We don't complete worthwhile projects.
- We express anger in destructive ways.
- We diminish others through sarcasm.
- We avoid those whom we are afraid to confront.
- We spread rumors on Facebook.

- We neglect communicating with our friends and relatives.
- We break promises and resolutions, even the ones that we make to ourselves.

The good news is: God loves us so much that He made a way for our relationship with Father-God could to be restored; this gives us the power to overcome the sin nature. This gift is called salvation. What we must understand and do to receive this gift is the topic of my next chapter.

# 6

# Transplanted into Healthy Soil

> For he has rescued us from the dominion of darkness
> and brought us into the kingdom of the Son he loves.
> —Colossians 1:13 (NIV)

The apple tree that my husband planted in the front yard of our village lot was of hearty rootstock; yet, as I explained earlier in this book, it did not prosper because we planted it too close to the curb. Whenever the village snowplow drove past our yard it drenched the tree and the soil around it with salt. This happened almost every day during some of our winter months. The salt-contaminated soil poisoned our apple tree. After five years it had only a few scrawny branches and leaves. It looked like it was dying, and it probably would have died if we had left it in that soil.

When we moved to our current location, we transplanted our apple tree into soil that was much healthier, and we located it farther from the road. Now our tree is tall—it has branched out, has more greenery, and looks healthy. We hope to harvest some apples next fall.

## A Necessary Transplant

*To help you understand the following concepts, please refer to the <u>Transplanted into Healthy Soil</u> diagram <u>(Image 3, page 181)</u> in the Appendix.*

Living in the contaminated soil of the sin nature, we can't develop into the beautiful and fruitful person God designed us to become. If we want to grow and prosper, then we, like that scrawny apple tree, must be transplanted into healthy soil.

Just as a tree cannot pull its roots out of toxic soil and move to a new location neither can we pull our roots out of the poisonous soil of the sin nature that we're stuck in—even though our choice to turn away from God was what placed us there. That's where Jesus comes in.

He has the power to pull us away from the grasp of the sin nature and transplant us into the healthy soil of his kingdom. That's why he came to earth. As we sink our roots into the soil of his love, we receive his transforming power and begin to produce healthy, good-tasting fruit such as self-control, joy, patience, and peace. This is the way Eugene Peterson, author of *The Message*, describes being transplanted: "God rescued us . . . He's set us up in the kingdom of the Son . . . the Son who got us out of the pit we were in, got rid of the sins we were doomed to keep repeating" (Colossians 1:13–14).

## Cooperation Needed

We don't arrive in God's kingdom by our own effort, yet it's not an automatic transfer. And even though we feel miserable, some of us choose to stay right where we are. For the transfer to occur, we must recognize that we need help and want the help that we need. Knowing we need help and wanting to receive it are two separate choices.

The truth is: we might be hanging on to our destructive desires and unhealthy emotional choices because sometimes they bring us benefits such as these:

- We enjoy getting revenge.

- We feel satisfaction when we nurse a grudge.
- We like the feeling of power we have when we intimidate others by exploding at them.
- When we hide feelings of envy and jealousy, we don't believe that we are hurting anyone.
- We do not want to give up *guilt* because what then would we have to motivate us?

Until we recognize that giving in to such desires will ultimately kill us, we won't change direction. That's where God comes in. He convinces us of the danger we're in by letting us continue down the wrong road until we feel some painful consequences. Frequently he brings along a friend, family member, neighbor or employer to help him make his point.

God might also take away some of our props. One of my life-long props has been ice cream. Early in my life, I learned how to stuff my anger and relieve both anxiety and guilt by filling my stomach with ice cream. Now, I can't eat even a spoonful without feeling yucky. No more using it to cover up unpleasant or embarrassing emotions! Unfortunately, I've found other foods that work just as well. But the relief I have when I stuff my emotions in that way quickly fades away.

When we love and cling to destructive desires and emotions, we destroy not only ourselves but also God's beautiful and perfect order. He will hold us accountable for our destructive choices. It's only when we realize how our choices have affected *God* and feel grieved about how we've offended him that we are truly motivated to change. Then, we face another choice—the choice of placing our faith in Jesus or on positive thinking and self-reform.

## Insufficient Efforts

Positive thinking and self-reform remind me of *The Little Engine that Could* story that I read to my children when they were younger. This story is about a little engine that needed to climb a high mountain. By repeating the phrase "I think I can" it succeeded in its mission. What we think about ourselves *does* affect our ability to perform, and there is a sense in which we all need self-confidence. However, our self-confidence needs to be based on an accurate measure of who we are and what we *can* do instead of some delusional notion that we're invincible.

Neither positive thinking nor having faith in ourselves is strong enough to free us from the power of the sin nature. If that were true, God (in the form of Jesus) would not have descended to earth.

## Perfect Performance

Jesus lived in a human body like ours and was tempted in all the ways that we are. But unlike us, he never met any desire or expressed any emotion in ways destructive and contrary to his Father's purpose. He completely trusted his Father and obeyed him in every situation.

When confronted by Satan, Jesus rejected every lie that Satan threw at him—

- The lie that would have driven him to make his physical desires and needs a higher priority than his relationship with his Father
- The lie that would have pushed him into defying the limitations that he had accepted from his Father
- The lie that would have caused him to set himself up as ruler of the universe before his Father's appointed time.

He's the only human ever born into this world who lived a perfect life—functional in every way. Yet, he died like a criminal—nailed to a tree. Why did he consent to such an unjust and cruel death? What did it accomplish? Long before he arrived on earth, God revealed the purpose of Jesus' death to his prophet, Isaiah, who explained it in this way:

> But he took our suffering on him
> and felt our pain for us.
> We saw his suffering
> and thought God was punishing him.
> But he was wounded for the wrong we did;
> he was crushed for the evil we did.
> The punishment, which made us well, was given to him,
> and we are healed because of his wounds.
> We all have wandered away like sheep;
> each of us has gone his own way.
> But the LORD has put on him the punishment
> for all the evil we have done.
> —Isaiah 53:4–6 (NCV)

God the Father accepted Jesus' death as a sufficient payment for our wrongdoings (sins) so that our relationship with him could be restored, and we could receive the power to live as he meant for us to live. When we finally break through denial, recognize how dysfunctional we are, remove the masks we wear, share our hidden pain, and admit how helpless we are to make changes, we are ready to receive this wonderful gift of forgiveness, freedom, and power.

Death is final. There will be no opportunity to come back and do things differently, even if we wish we could. The hope Jesus offers is not wishful thinking. We can know for certain that we will go to heaven. We are made acceptable to God through Jesus. This is a reliable promise; it's based on the fact that God raised Jesus from the dead. Jesus' resurrection is the evidence that God accepted Jesus sacrificial death a sufficient payment for the judgment we deserved.

"This is how much God loved the world: He gave his Son, his one and only Son. And this is why: so that no one need be destroyed; by believing in him, anyone can have a whole and lasting life" (John 3:16 MSG). When we believe that Jesus is God and that he died on our behalf, trust him, and turn our lives over to his control, the transfer into his kingdom is complete. However, it's just the first step to becoming the healthy "Oaks of Righteousness" we are meant to become.

Although (as I said earlier) we have been transplanted into healthy soil, the sin nature doesn't disappear. We can easily fall into our old destructive emotional patterns, and that makes growing into emotional and spiritual maturity a challenging process—the topic of my next chapter.

# 7

# A Dynamic Dance with the Gardener

> Live in me. Make your home in me just as I do in you. In the same way that a branch can't bear grapes by itself but only by being joined to the vine, you can't bear fruit unless you are joined with me . . . Make yourselves at home in my love.
> —John 15:4, 9 (MSG)

As a child, I often dreamt about my wedding day—imagining the beautiful white dress I would wear and picturing the huge bouquet of roses mixed with lilies of the valley I would carry as I walked down the aisle on my father's arm. During my college days several of my friends chose me to be one of their bridesmaids, my sister chose me to be her maid of honor, and my brother asked me to sing at his wedding, but *my* Prince Charming did not show up. To make things worse, whenever I went home my grandmother said, "Jane, haven't you met any nice fellows yet? Don't you *want* to get married?" She also suggested the names of several eligible farmers in the area.

Finally, the summer I turned twenty-eight, I took some initiative and applied for a job at a Christian camp. I hoped I would meet someone there who'd be looking for someone as intelligent, kind, spiritually sensitive, and mature as I was. After I'd been there for about a month and had no dates or prospective ones, I poured out my heart to God saying something like this: "You know how lonely I am, Lord.

You know how much I want a husband. I believe it's a good desire. I believe you gave it to me. I don't understand why I haven't met anyone who loves me, but I know that you love me. If your plan for me does not include marriage, then please make me content to live a single life. Teach me to find more joy in my relationship with you. Help me become satisfied with your love." After that, an amazing peace filled my heart, and I gave up my search for a husband.

A few weeks later when a new man arrived at camp, I was *not* wondering if this was the guy for me. Though he *was* the one God had picked for me, my future husband did not show up until I quit looking and trusted God to meet my deepest love needs. He gave me a man who also depends on God to meet the love needs of his heart. John's love for me is an overflow of the love that he receives from God. I'm thankful for this because it did not take long after we were married for me to discover that I wasn't as kind and mature as I thought I was. John also had some growing to do.

Though we were Christians, the sin nature in both of us showed up. Outbursts of anger, feelings of guilt, deep anxiety, hidden resentment, envy, and other destructive passions saddened us and made the early days of our marriage difficult. We prayed for help and God heard us. He showed us that we needed to cultivate our relationship with the Holy Spirit—whom Jesus sends to those who receive him as Savior and Lord.

## The Promised Helper

*To help you understand the following concepts, please refer to the We Must Choose Our Dance Partner diagram (Image 4, page 182) in the Appendix.*

This is Jesus' promise: "I will talk to the Father, and he'll provide you another Friend so that you will always have someone with you. This Friend is the Spirit of Truth" (John 14:16 MSG).

The Spirit of Truth is the one who inspired and instructed writers of the Bible. When I read the words that they wrote down, inviting that same Spirit to instruct and inspire me, I discover what I'm really like. He shows me the destructive lies and painful feelings that I've hidden in my heart. Because he speaks with compassion and gentleness, I don't feel discouraged. This Friend teaches me all things and reminds me of things Jesus said—the words of Scripture. He comforts me by making me aware of Jesus' presence.

As I remain with him in a relationship of trust and submission, he produces the fruit of righteousness in me—"love, joy, peace, patience, kindness, goodness, faithfulness, gentleness, and self-control" (Galatians 5:22–23 NIV). That's a description of the character of Christ. As I chose to obey him, Jesus' nature becomes my nature. What a contrast this is to the destructive passions of the sin nature!

This is a simple example of how the Holy Spirit produces fruit in my life. Currently, I am on a restricted diet. Included on the list of foods I *cannot* have is ice cream. Though I've known for years that it makes me sick, I've continued to eat it. My husband eats ice cream almost every day. Sometimes, when I've seen him enjoying a large bowl of ice cream, I've reacted with envy and resentment; I've secretly pulled a half-gallon of peanut butter cup ice cream from the freezer and helped myself to a generous serving. During those occasions, no matter how much I've eaten, I've never felt satisfied.

Yesterday, however, I felt and acted differently. I said to my husband, "Would you like me to bring you a dish of ice cream?" I made this offer without any envy or resentment in my heart, and I felt satisfied and content watching him eat what I did not have. For several weeks, I've been able to stick to the entire diet my doctor gave me without feeling envious or resentful when I'm in the presence of people who are eating the foods which I normally enjoy. That is a huge change. It's evidence of the Holy Spirit's presence and power in me.

I can't explain exactly *how* the Holy Spirit grows fruit in our lives. It's a mystery. It happens when we are living in an obedient, trusting relationship with Jesus Christ. His Spirit lives in us and speaks truth to our hearts. He doesn't usually speak in an audible voice; it's more like a thought—but not something we would have thought of. In order to hear the voice of the Spirit, we need to invite him to speak to us. Then we need to listen.

Who would not want to remain in a close relationship with Jesus? I deeply want to; however, that's not an automatic certainty for any of us. Our everyday choices determine what our relationship with him will look like. As I mentioned in the previous chapter, the sin nature does not go away when God transfers us to his kingdom. We must continually reject its lies and replace them with truth.

## The Dance

Jesus does not compel us to obey him. He empowers us to overcome evil and destructive passions, but it does not happen *automatically*. It's a shared effort. Eugene Peterson, in *The Message*, uses the phrase (Matthew 11:28–30) to describe the shared relationship that Jesus invites us to have with him.

I love that "unforced rhythms of grace" phrase. It reminds me of a dance. I'm not a great dancer. My least well-developed intelligence is kinesthetic. When I was in college, I had to take beginning swimming twice in order to pass it. Kinesthetic intelligence is one of my husband's highest developed abilities. He loves to dance. I love watching him dance. We do it as a part of our worship on Sunday mornings. I managed to dance with him at our daughters' weddings without crushing his toes.

The concept of dancing with God delights me. I call this dance with Jesus "Choosing Grace." It has two basic steps—grace and responsibility. Grace is God's step of love toward me. Responsibility is my step of love toward God. Jesus said, "If you keep my commands, you'll remain intimately at home in my love" (John 15:10 MSG).

Choosing grace is about dancing in such a close relationship with Jesus that his nature becomes a part of us, motivating our decisions and empowering our behavioral changes. Here is a clear Biblical statement describing the interaction between grace and responsibility: "Continue to work out your salvation with fear and trembling, for it is God who works in you to will and to act according to his good purpose" (Philippians 2:12–13 NIV).

Choosing grace is about *acting* on our decisions so that our behavior will change. However, it's much more than a how-to-do list for selecting and practicing new behaviors. Through this dynamic dance with Jesus we are transformed, and we become like him. How do responsibility and grace work together to bring about character change and freedom from destructive desires and emotions? There are two common misunderstandings.

## Problems on the Dance Floor

Some of us focus entirely on God's grace, and others of us focus entirely on our responsibility. Some of us depend on God to do all the dancing, while others of us leave him standing on the dance floor and take off in our own independent rhythm.

When we place responsibility—as well as grace—totally in God's lap, our slogan becomes "let go and let God." God did not design us as robots, and he does not bypass our will. We have the responsibility of choosing whether or not we will rely on God's empowering grace. When we place responsibility on our shoulders and forget about grace we take up the "just-say-no!" slogan. Our program of self-reform does not usually work very well or last very long. The only way we can be successful by just saying no to our destructive desires is by lying to ourselves—overlooking our slip-ups.

On any day, I may deceive myself into thinking I can stay away from the chocolate ice cream which gives me digestive problems. Perhaps by God's grace I've been successful for a few weeks. Now, I think my will power is sufficient. I no longer need God's assistance. What happens? I'm so focused on my performance that my craving takes over.

I tend to swing from one end of the spectrum to the other. Sometimes, I act as if God is totally responsible for my growth. In passive *irresponsibility*, I refuse to take initiative. I don't anticipate problems, and I don't plan *how* I can obey. I sing "I want what God wants" while waiting for *him* to exercise the will he gave to *me*. What's the result? Nothing happens. Why doesn't this work?

God will neither take over my will nor override the choices I make. His freedom of choice gift includes responsibility to act and accountability for our action or failure to act. The simplest example of responsibility I can think of is the following story.

When my daughter was in kindergarten, she enjoyed listening to Aunt Bertha stories. One story was about a little girl who complained because God would not answer her prayer.

> "What did you pray?" her mother asked.
> "I asked God to tie my shoe lace."

What did my daughter learn from the story? God would not tie her shoelace, but someone else might. And she found a friend who would do it.

The cliché "God won't do for us what we can do for ourselves" is true, and we might add this one: "God will not credit us when we do things for others which they can do for themselves." That kind of

*Emotional Freedom*

help is unhelpful and can lead us into a co-dependent relationship. God will not be our co-dependent. He offers us empowering grace, but he never disrespects and strips us of dignity by doing things for us that we can do for ourselves. At times I've felt disappointed about that, thinking how much easier life would be if God would perform a miracle and set me free.

When we are choosing, day-by-day, to live in a close relationship with Jesus—relying on his favor, depending on him to do for us what we cannot do for ourselves, and trusting him to meet our needs—God's grace empowers us so that we can overcome our destructive and addictive desires and emotions.

Donna is learning that in order to have intimacy with Jesus, there are things that she must do to facilitate the dance. She invites you to make your heart a home for Jesus:

> You can invite Jesus to make your heart his home. But you must make the home ready for him. (Just like learning to tie your shoes.) You need to change your way of living so it is pleasing to Jesus. The way you think and the company you keep. How you feel and what you do for your family. Change what you read and what you do for entertainment. Make it pleasing for him. He will stay in your home, so be a good host and don't ignore him. Sit with him and have long talks. Tell him what is bothering you—what makes you happy or what makes you sad. He is a good listener and wants to hear from you. He loves you and wants to be asked to help. Sit quietly and listen to him speak. He will help you bear any burden. There are none too small, nor too big. He, the great I AM, King of Kings, Lord of Lords, and God of All *can handle it!*

We can rely on God with confidence because he keeps his promises. He gave us the things he promised to give us, fulfilling all the prophecies of the Old Testament. He gives us everything we need for well-being and the development of godly character so that we can live a life pleasing to him and find joy in our relationship with him. I like the way Peter explains this truth— "God made great and marvelous promises, so that his nature would become part of us. Then we could escape our evil desires and the corrupt influences of this world" (2 Peter 1:4 CEV).

No one becomes a skilled dancer overnight. But even if we are awkward and slow, Jesus will teach us how to dance. We will progress faster and more easily if we learn and practice certain disciplines. I will discuss six essential ones in the following chapter.

# 8

# Nutrients for Growth

> God has given us the Disciplines of the spiritual life as a means of receiving grace. The Disciplines allow us to place ourselves before God so that he can transform us.
>
> —Richard Foster[1]

I'd like to have more vacations. I'd like to sit on my deck for longer periods of time—watching the movement of the water in the lake below, listening to the birds, taking photos of my flowers or simply soaking in the sunshine. I'd like to spontaneously drop in on some of my friends and enjoy a cup of tea or just chat. I'd like to sleep-in more often. My husband says, "You're retired. Why don't you do these things?"

I could do more of those things but I choose not to. Instead, most mornings I get up early and do my Bible study and prayer journaling. Then, after breakfast, I sit back down at my computer and begin writing. Except for a few necessary breaks, I stay there until lunchtime. (When I look out the window and see the lake looking unusually beautiful, I do sneak in a photo.)

I can't say that I always like disciplining myself in this way, but I like the result: God is transforming my emotional life, and I have an increased measure of joy, peace, and self-control.

Discipline by itself does not make us more Christ-like. It's simply the things we do to demonstrate our dependence on God. It's embracing Jesus. We offer our bodies to him, so that he can work in and through us. Eugene Peterson explains it this way:

> So here's what I want you to do, God helping you: Take your everyday, ordinary life—your sleeping, eating, going-to-work, and walking-around life—and place it before God as an offering. Embracing what God does for you is the best thing you can do for him. Don't become so well-adjusted to your culture that you fit into it without even thinking. Instead, fix your attention on God. You'll be changed from the inside out. Readily recognize what he wants from you, and quickly respond to it. Unlike the culture around you, always dragging you down to its level of immaturity, God brings the best out of you, develops well-formed maturity in you.
> —Romans 12: 1–5 (MSG)

In this chapter I present six disciplines. If you want to benefit from the material in the rest of the book, then I recommend that you practice them. They will prepare you to successfully make the choices that you will be challenged to make as you read upcoming chapters on the topics of anger, resentment and revenge.

## Bible Study

I place Bible study first on the list because we tend to neglect it in our daily life. Jesus placed a high value on Scripture. When he was tempted by Satan to make bread out of a stone, he responded with these words: "It takes more than bread to stay alive. It takes a steady stream of words from God's mouth" (Matthew 4:4 MSG).

How many of us would skip breakfast or lunch or dinner every day for a week? We feed our bodies. We must also feed our spirits. Is opening up our Bibles once a day too much for us to expect of ourselves? I've been reading and studying Scripture since I was a teen-ager. From years of experience, I know it's a necessary part of my daily spiritual diet. It's as important as breathing. Every day, I invite God to speak to me through the Scripture that I read, and the Holy Spirit gives me a personal message to focus on.

(If it's easier for you to learn by hearing rather than by reading, then you can listen to an audio Bible. By reading several versions of the Bible and comparing them, you can gain a rich understanding. Bible Gateway.com[2] offers free access to numerous versions.)

In his letter to a young Christian, Paul said, "Every part of Scripture is God-breathed and useful one way or another—showing us truth, exposing our rebellion, correcting our mistakes, training us to live God's way. Through the Word we are put together and shaped up for the tasks God has for us" (2 Timothy 3:16 MSG).

The Apostle Peter said, "No prophecy of Scripture is of any private interpretation, for prophecy never came by the will of man, but holy men of God spoke *as they were* moved by the Holy Spirit" (2 Peter 1:20–21 NKJV). This means that the people who wrote the Bible did not come up with their own ideas about what God is like and how he wants us to live—the Holy Spirit taught them.

When we read the Bible, it's important for us to ask the same Holy Spirit to teach us. He will give us understanding of the concepts and show us how the truths of Scripture apply to our specific situations. But we must do our part. This means diligent study; we pay attention to details, ask questions, meditate—think about the Scripture that we read, discuss it with others, and memorize it. Most importantly, we must put Scriptural principles into practice by doing what God tells us to do. This is called obedience.

## Faith-motivated Obedience

With the following words, Jesus warned his disciples about the danger of hearing *his* words and *not* putting them into practice:

> So why do you keep calling me 'Lord, Lord!' when you don't do what I say? I will show you what it's like when someone comes to me, listens to my teaching, and then follows it. It is like a person building a house who digs deep and lays the foundation on solid rock. When the floodwaters rise and break against that house, it stands firm because it is well built. But anyone who hears and doesn't obey is like a person who builds a house without a foundation. When the floods sweep down against that house, it will collapse into a heap of ruins.
> —Luke 6:46–49 NLT)

Obedience is not a popular word in the culture where we live. We like to think that we are independent, and we do not want anyone to tell us what to do—especially if we are adults. Children might need instruction, but we can think for ourselves. Some of us think obedience means that we throw away our minds and never say "no" to anyone or anything. Obeying God does not mean that we give up thinking. It means that we recognize how limited our knowledge is and how much we need God's wisdom. Obeying God is a natural response when we believe the following things: God is all powerful, beautiful, wise, and good; he loves us and his plans for us will bring us eternal joy; he is trustworthy and will keep his promises.

Since we can't see God, believing these things about him requires faith. Many people mistakenly think that they don't have faith because they don't feel anything, but faith is *not* a feeling; faith is a conviction—a belief. It's being certain that something is true and acting on that certainty. Faith is "confidence in what we hope for and assurance about what we do not see . . . [and] without faith it is impossible to please God, because anyone who comes to him must believe that he exists and that he rewards those who earnestly seek him" (Hebrews (11: 1 and 6 NIV).

Faith in God means we trust him. Trust motivates us to do the things that he tells us to do—to live according to the guidelines he set down for us. How can we remember what he tells us to do? It can be helpful to write his words (Scripture) in a journal and pray them into our lives.

## Prayer-journaling

Prayer is our primary way of connecting with Jesus. It's not a complicated thing; it's simply having a conversation with God. It's meant to be two-way communication in which we speak to God, and then we listen for his response. Usually, we don't need as much instruction about speaking to God as we do hearing from God. Most often his response is "a still small voice." We can pray silently or out loud. Even if we only lift our thoughts up to God, we are praying.

Prayer-journaling is simply placing our prayer on paper. Perhaps, you don't like to write, believe you can't write, or feel intimidated by writing; don't let those factors keep you from learning this discipline. I've practiced it for many years. I sit down at a table with my notebook and tell Jesus about my thoughts and feelings. Jesus already knows what they are; I don't do this to inform him. I do this to become honest with myself. When I place my resentment, envy, anxiety, revenge, guilt, and other destructive desires and emotions on paper, I have to *face* these feelings. I can't pretend everything is fine.

Prayer journaling can be scary. Sometimes it stirs up painful memories that have strong feelings associated with them. This hidden pain could be fueling our destructive emotional patterns; to become free we need to face it. When we trust him with our secrets and invite him to come into our pain, we discover God's compassion and find healing. When we feel like giving up, he gives us the courage to continue our journey.

Placing our thoughts and feelings on paper and presenting them to God is one part of prayer journaling. The other part is finding out what God thinks about our thoughts and feelings.

Along with the thoughts and feelings that I record in my journal, I include questions that come to my mind. Then, I quietly listen to hear what God has to say to me. He speaks to me in various says. Sometimes he gives me a picture; I see it in my mind. Frequently, a phrase from Scripture pops up in my mind. Sometimes it's a song. I write down what I believe God is saying to me; then, to make sure that my thought is actually from God, I check it out with what the Bible teaches. God never says anything that contradicts Scripture.

Jesus is the Person of Truth. The Bible is his written word to us; therefore, it also is truth. The following Psalm of David describes the value of God's word:

> The instructions of the Lord are perfect,
>   reviving the soul.
> The decrees of the Lord are trustworthy,
>   making wise the simple.
> The commandments of the Lord are right,
>   bringing joy to the heart.
> The commands of the Lord are clear,
>   giving insight for living.
> Reverence for the Lord is pure,
>   lasting forever.
> The laws of the Lord are true;
>   each one is fair.

> They are more desirable than gold,
>   even the finest gold.
> They are sweeter than honey,
>   even honey dripping from the comb.
> They are a warning to your servant,
>   a great reward for those who obey them.
>
> —Psalm 19:7–11 (NLT)

When we do not know what Jesus thinks and wants, we are unable to obey him. When we do not obey him, we lose the joy of his companionship and are powerless to control our destructive desires. All our efforts produce nothing. When we talk to him and listen to him throughout the day, he transforms our thinking. Gradually, as our beliefs become lined up with his truth, our values, desires, and feelings change, and we produce a harvest of good fruit: love, joy, peace, patience, goodness, kindness, faithfulness, gentleness and self-control.

In the following paragraph, Donna shares the transformation that occurred in her life as the result of prayer journaling.

> Your love, Lord, is like a soft warm blanket to snuggle in, to keep out the cold. The blanket doesn't warm me immediately; I have to wrap it around myself. I have to stay in it awhile. And, it has taken time for me to feel your love. But now, I am as comfortable in your gentle love as I am in a soft blanket. I am growing every day. I learn something new and experience new ways to serve you that I had not known. Before I began prayer-journaling, I feel I was a very envious person. I was envious of someone's talent to sing, or another's looks, and yet, someone else's faith. I felt I was not good enough. I see, now, Lord, no one is perfect. We are all growing, and I am OK! I can see and recognize some of the blessings you have put in

my life. I can see and recognize the talents you have given me.

Experiencing this kind of transformation in our lives will produce gratitude and joy. It's important to express our gratitude to God through worship.

## Truth-inspired Worship

Truth-inspired worship helps us take our eyes off of ourselves and focus them on God. When we are struggling with painful emotions, we desperately need (for at least a few moments) to take our eyes off of ourselves. We may not think so. We might resist it. And we may not know how to do it. But it is possible.

We can learn to focus outside of our pain and to intentionally focus our thoughts on truth—on Jesus. He is Truth. This will bring healing to our spirits—but that's only a side benefit. If our motivation for worshipping God is to be healed and/or to feel good, we are not really worshipping God. We are not giving anything to him. We are asking him for something. He is not a celestial Santa Claus or a magician. True worship is about giving something to God.

We must take our eyes off of ourselves when we worship because worshipping God is not for *us*. It's for *him*. Yes, we do gain benefits, but they are secondary. God comes to us in a special way when his children praise him. In the following paragraph, Crystal shares what her worship experience is like.

> Worshiping God with music is my favorite way to worship. When I sing to God and play my piano, I feel His loving presence in such a tender, real way. He speaks to me, encourages me, guides my prayers and changes my perspective. One of my favorite songs

is: "Turn Your Eyes upon Jesus." The chorus reads: "Turn your eyes upon Jesus, Look full in His wonderful face; And the things of earth will grow strangely dim In the light of His glory and grace." This describes my worship experience. When I worship, my focus is no longer on myself or others; my attention is on Jesus. In comparison to His glory, everyone and everything in my life pales. My world grows dim, His Kingdom brightens.

In Old Testament days, before Jesus came to earth, God's way of showing up when his people offered praise was a little different than it is today. He came in a visible cloud or a pillar of fire. His people felt awe and joy. His presence filled them with confidence. Psalm 22 describes someone feeling abandoned by God. The people around him are mocking him and making fun of his faith in God. In the middle of it all, he chooses to praise God.

Today, when we praise God his presence still comes but not usually in a visible way. Still, we can feel his presence. And it's a wonderful calming feeling. We feel high. But if we get caught up in the feeling too much we can become emotionally addicted. What happens when that feeling we love is not there the next time that we worship? We might sing the same song but not feel excited about it. What do we do then?

We decide our worship experience has failed us. Perhaps we should visit another church where the music is louder and the worship time is longer. We might go there. It's great for a while. Then, that feeling we are looking for disappears—again, so we go somewhere else.

Worship is not about our feeling good. It's about expressing gratitude to God for how good he is. It's not filling up our empty emotional buckets, it's about praising him. However, he does fill our empty buckets when we start expressing our gratitude and begin praising him for who he is. Those good feelings might not be present immediately, but if we look long enough and hard enough at God, then we will eventually experience joy. In his presence our spirits and souls are refreshed and restored. Yet even when we don't experience joy, we must choose to praise him, because he deserves it.

## Restorative Rest

Facing and working through our emotional conflicts takes energy, a lot of energy—and time. It can be exhausting. Breaking through denial and facing the magnitude of the consequences of our emotional addictions is painful. Learning new behaviors requires discipline. If we are not careful, we can become so intense in our healing journey that we burnout.

We emotion-driven people do not know how to rest. We may know how to escape into pleasure, but that's not true rest. It might temporarily feel good, but it does not restore us. True rest restores us. It refreshes and strengthens our spirits, souls, and bodies.

Currently, I am connected with an online group of writers. For twenty five days, we committed ourselves to write every day—scheduling in as much time as we possibly can to do it. For the past nine days, I've worked very hard. This morning I had planned to write a minimum of three hours. When I woke up, however, I felt exhausted.

My mind was still processing feelings connected to a difficult (but good) decision that I had made last night. I knew it would not be productive for me to go straight to my computer. My mind felt too tired for intensive thought. My body felt hungry. I fixed myself a nutritious breakfast and ate it slowly. Then, I spent a few minutes gazing at the reflections in the lake. It was 10:00 a.m. by the time that I finally sat down at my computer. I've been pushing myself hard. Today I may not write more than 45 minutes. That's okay.

*Emotional Freedom*

The Lord reminded me of Psalm 127, which tell us it's useless to work from early morning until late at night. He doesn't intend us to become workaholics.

I have a strong tendency in that direction. It began in childhood. My parents were hard working farmers who grew up in the years called the Great Depression. They received no government subsidy if their crops failed. No unemployment or disability insurance, no social security and no Medicare benefits. They worked hard every day of the week—until Sunday. Sunday was the Sabbath, which they always observed. They rested their bodies and rested their souls. In the morning, they went to church; there, they met with the Lord and with friends whom they often invited to join them for Sunday dinner. In the afternoons, they often took naps. Later on, they played board games.

Those activities may have been restful for my parents, but they were not restful for me. Games meant competition. Church meant sitting still. Neither nursery nor childcare was available. Because my younger brother wouldn't sit still in church, my parents often asked my sister and me to take him to a nearby park. Our job was to protect him and keep him out of trouble. That involved responsibility. It's taken me years to find what is restful for me—what restores my soul.

When I'm tired I do not get recharged by going to a party. I get recharged by taking a long walk. I prefer to go by myself. Solitude strengthens me. I am what you call an "introvert." I am also a highly sensitive person. I can't take a lot of stimulation. On the Myers-Briggs Personality Inventory (one measurement of introversion), my introversion scored in the highest four per cent of the population. A football party at my house exhausts me.

Each one of us need to find out what brings us refreshment, and then arrange our schedules so that we can do what we need to do to be renewed. I love music but I don't like to listen to CD's or YouTube videos because I get frustrated. Even with my hearing aids, I can't understand the words.

All of us—being spirit-creatures, not just physical bodies—need to pay attention to our inner world. And to help us maintain these five disciplines we need someone "with skin on" to help keep us accountable on our journey.

## Grace-filled Accountability

We need to find a person who is a bit more mature than we are who will hold us accountable: facilitate our honesty, challenge us about keeping our commitments, and encourage us in our journey. This, of course, involves trust. It's important to find someone who is worthy of our trust.

In their book *Safe People* Henry Cloud and John Townsend describe unsafe (untrustworthy) people and contrast them with safe (trustworthy) people. The following list combines their criteria with my insights.

- Unsafe people avoid closeness; they are not "real."
- Safe people are empathetic and appropriately transparent about their own struggles.
- Unsafe people try to control us; they resist our freedom.
- Safe people respect our boundaries and encourage us to make our own decisions.
- Unsafe people flatter us.
- Safe people confront us with gentleness; they help us think through what the consequence of our decisions might be.
- Unsafe people condemn us.
- Safe people forgive us, pray for us, and stay with us.
- Unsafe are a negative influence on us; they bring out the worst in us.

- Safe people are a positive influence on us; they encourage us to be our best.
- Unsafe people are emotionally unstable, unreliable, and unpredictable.
- Safe people are emotionally mature, dependable, and consistent in their behavior.
- Unsafe people gossip.
- Safe people keep confidences.[3]

We need to have a relationship with someone who will facilitate our honesty, challenge, and encourage us, but we don't need someone who is out to fix us—telling us exactly *what* to do, exactly *when* to do it, and exactly *how* to do it. That destroys our sense of competency.

We need someone who will encourage *us* to take initiative: make choices, evaluate them with wisdom, design, and follow through with a next step. We need a cheerleader who gets excited about our progress, a coach who helps us recognize the smartest next play, a nutritionist who will teaches us to analyze the "food" we are eating, and a farther-along friend who admits to not yet being perfect.

Obviously, no one person can do all of these things. Accountability works most effectively in a group setting, where there's a mutual commitment to growth and an atmosphere of acceptance.

God has given me many partners as I've walked this journey. One of them is my husband and soul mate, John. After forty-seven years we are still in love. It's a much more mature kind of love than we started out with. Still, John tends to be a fixer. He loves me so much that it upsets him when I hurt. He knows he can't fix it; but he wants to. That frustrates me; it's not helpful. Besides that, he's a man and I'm a woman. I need to have other women to share with, and he needs men in his life. During the time I was deeply depressed, I needed the help of a counselor.

Having these six disciplines—Bible study, faith-motivated obedience, prayer-journaling, truth-inspired worship, restorative rest, and grace-filled accountability—in place is necessary for our success in overcoming destructive desires and emotions. Before you go on to the second part of my book, describing in detail the destructive emotional patterns of anger, resentment, and revenge, as well as alternative healthy choices, I suggest you find someone who will help you learn and began to practice these disciplines.

# PART THREE

# Attain FREEDOM—Make the Necessary Choices

# 9

# Identify Dysfunctional Anger

> When we're angry, we have enormous power available . . . what we choose to do with that power can move us like a missile to a place of resolution and peace or to the point of destruction.
>
> —Neil Clark Warren[1]

In his book *Make Anger Your Ally,* Dr. Warren explains that all of us have the God-given capacity for anger. He explains it in this way:

> Anger is a physical state of readiness. When we are angry, we are prepared to act. Physiologically, what happens is this: More adrenaline is secreted, more sugar is released, our hearts beat faster, our blood pressure rises, and the pupils of our eye open wide. We are highly alert. So when we are angry, all of the power of our person is available to us. This, and this alone is anger. Preparedness. Power.[2]

Yet some people believe that any expression of anger is wrong. Denial seems the perfect solution for such a dilemma. That's the way we handled anger in my family of origin. My mother lived to be ninety; yet in all those years, she never (to my knowledge) said that she felt angry.

After I graduated from college, I saw her infrequently, so I suppose it's possible that I missed something. I remember times during my growing-up years when mother got disturbed or "upset" (as my father put it) over the antics of my younger brother. My father chuckled and at the same time warned me not to act naughty like my brother did. "Don't upset your mother" was a command and warning that I took seriously.

Looking back as an adult, I suspect my father feared my mother's anger and possibly his own. Through the family grapevine, I learned that he suffered physical beatings—the result of parental tempers. By denying his anger Dad may have been trying to protect his family from the kind of abuse he'd experienced. He was not physically abusive, but he became very critical of himself.

Since my parents did not talk about or admit to anger, I wrongly assumed they were never angry. And because they were very religious people—and people who truly loved God—I implicitly connected all expressions of anger with sin (dysfunctional behavior). I believed anger would always result in separation from others and from God. I thought that it would at all times destroy relationships.

The Bible does not say that anger *itself* is wrong. With the following statement, the Apostle Paul made it clear that anger is sin only when we express it in destructive ways: "Go ahead and be angry. You do well to be angry—but don't use your anger as fuel for revenge. And don't stay angry. Don't go to bed angry" (Ephesians 4:26 MSG). Anger results in sin if we ignore it, let it accumulate, and/or express it in ways that injure ourselves and others.

Because on rare occasions I had seen my father explode, I eventually admitted to myself that he did possess feelings of anger. Most of the time, he internalized anger and got depressed, and I followed his example—burying and denying my anger until my mid-twenties. Finally, at that point, I was so depressed that I contemplated suicide.

My family believed that depression was a shameful condition, and suicide was more shameful. So I did not tell them what was going on nor did I go to them for help. But I was desperate for help, so I sought counsel. After six months of counseling, I begin to identify and own my angry feelings.

I believed that anger was a bad emotion, and I was deeply afraid of it. Along with my family I thought that violence was the only way of expressing anger. To be safe I denied the *fact* of my anger. To avoid conflict I hid my true thoughts and feelings. When we deny the fact of our anger, it shows up in other forms such as depression, sarcasm, or ill health.

God gets angry, but he always expresses his anger in appropriate ways—with unerring wisdom, immense patience, great compassion, and perfect justice. As the Psalmist says, "The LORD shows mercy and is kind. He does not become angry quickly, and he has great love. He will not always accuse us, and he will not be angry forever" (103:8–9 NCV).

Because we have a limited perspective, are quick to jump-to-conclusions, and tend to be self-centered, we often express our anger in ways that are inappropriate and hurtful. Using our capacity to get angry for purposes other than the constructive way that God intended for us to use it is dysfunctional. God calls that dysfunction sin. Being unaware of our anger (as well as consciously covering it up) makes us unsafe people because we tend to unexpectedly express that hidden anger in hurtful ways. Knowing that we are angry (and admitting that we are) makes us safer to be around because it gives us an opportunity for self-control. The expression of anger does not have to be destructive; we can learn how to handle it in ways that result in improved communication and closer relationships.

By realizing that anger is an experience in which we make many choices, rather than an isolated event (an explosion), we can expand our understanding of it.

Understanding the <u>Map of Destructive Anger</u> diagram (**Image 5, page 183, in the Appendix**) gives us opportunities to (1) recognize the choices that we usually make in the development of anger, (2) determine whether those choices are contributing to health or to dysfunction and disease, (3) discard our unhealthy choices, and (4) start making healthier ones.

## Stage One: A Situation Becomes Unreasonable

Anger begins developing when a situation becomes unreasonable to us. Something is too offensive, unpleasant, wrong or painful for us to accept. We differ in our ideas of what is unreasonable. Some determining factors are personality, values, health, and maturity. I expect my two-year old grandson struggling with independence issues to become angry more frequently than his ten-year old cousin does. If we're recovering from an illness or surgery, we might become angry more quickly than someone experiencing good health. People whose happiness depends on the size of their bank account might become angrier when they are a victim of theft than those who are satisfied with the material goods that they have.

As I explained in chapter 3, emotions develop from our heart (root) beliefs. Beliefs based on lies produce unhealthy behavior (fruit). Beliefs based on truth produce healthy behavior (fruit). How we experience anger and what we are taught about it early in life shape our beliefs about anger.

In the Christian home where I grew up, I believed that I should accept everything. I should not feel offended in any situation that was unpleasant or hurt by any person that was unkind. It was my duty to accept unfairness and pain and to "turn the other cheek." This is what it meant to "carry my cross." I did not learn this entirely from the formal teaching that I had. I picked up much of it through my interpretation of life as I observed the behavior of both my family and early spiritual mentors. This was my motto:

> Nothing is too painful, nothing too unfair;
> For those who follow Jesus—there's a cross to bear.
> A display of anger would prove I have no faith;
> And Jesus does not answer a child who is irate.

If nothing was unreasonable, then I had no basis for anger. I was often angry, but I managed to hide it from everyone—including myself. Eventually, my desire for emotional health overcame my fear (and pride) of looking at my anger. I learned that Christians have a legitimate basis for anger and that we can learn to express it in self-controlled and constructive ways.

## Stage Two: Our Stress Level Builds

If an unreasonable situation is undetected, ignored, or unresolved, we experience stress. This means we have a surge of adrenaline which increases internal tension and prepares our bodies for action. Depending upon our personalities as well as our life experiences, we either fight or run away. When we are fatigued, ill, or for other reasons already stressed, we may choose to ignore the unreasonableness rather than to confront it. Doing this adds to the stress. Other factors which increase stress are (1) the common belief that others are responsible for our anger and/or (2) we lack the skills needed to handle feelings.

Some of us are not very well tuned-in to our bodies. We don't recognize the signs of stress until we get a wake-up call in the form of an illness or experience burnout. We might be what some psychologists call "A-Type personalities."

This is how Dr. Archibald Hart describes A-Type personalities:

- They have a high degree of competitiveness.
- They are easily irritated by delays.
- They have a low tolerance for frustration.
- They are hard-driving and ambitious.
- They are highly aggressive.
- They are easily angered and often have free-floating hostility.
- They cannot relax without feeling guilty.
- They are confident on the surface but insecure within.
- They speak aggressively, accentuating key words.
- They have a tendency to finish other people's sentences.[3]

God used Archibald Hart's book to help me recognize my A-Type tendencies. It offers very practical advice for change. Through reading it, God showed me what I am like when I disregard the needs of my physical body—particularly rest and exercise. Ignoring my physical needs reduces my ability to respond to unreasonable situations with grace and patience.

## Stage Three: We Explode (or Implode)

Stress ignored eventually leads to the third stage of anger: an explosion occurs. This explosion is proportional to the intensity of our stress. This phase of the process is what we generally call anger. Both verbal and physical abuse can occur if anger is intense. Uncontrolled expression of feelings often results in destructive patterns such as blaming, name calling, shouting, threatening, screaming, hitting, slapping, kicking, and shooting.

Outward expressions of anger don't have to be uncontrolled or destructive, but if we are unaware of other alternatives (or concerned about hurting others) then we might implode, that is: explode on the inside directing anger toward ourselves. We might do this through generating negative self-talk. Self-talk is the inner conversation that takes place in our minds.

For example, if we demand perfection from ourselves, then falling short of that standard will cause us to feel angry. Our self-talk might sound like this: "I'm stupid. I should have known better. I never do anything right. I deserve to be punished." Negative thoughts such as these affect our bodies, minds, souls, and spirits. Some of us might develop headaches; others of us develop stomach pain or tightness in our throats. I develop muscle tension.

Because I have chronic muscle pain and stiffness, I need to break up non-activity tasks with movement and limit the time I spend sitting and typing. Sometimes I feel frustrated about my limitations, but this only increases stress. By imploding, we might deceive not only others but also ourselves into thinking we are not even angry. This makes the resolution of issues much more difficult.

## Stage Four: We Need Distance

After we explode we need to give ourselves some time and space to recover. In this stage of the process we allow our bodies to regain equilibrium; our blood pressure decreases, our heart rate slows down, and we can think clearly once again. When we insist on resolving an issue while in the heat of emotion, we only produce more frustration. It's important to give ourselves, as well as others, the time and space that we need to calm down.

I wish that I'd understood this need for space during the time my youngest daughter was a pre-teen. Her anger along with her hormone levels fluctuated greatly. She would explode, run into her room, and close the door. I would run after her, pound on the door, and demand that we talk. I didn't realize that it was impossible for her to talk until she cooled down. On the other hand, if we don't set a limit on the distance that we need to cool down we will never resolve the original problem.

Depending on what we choose to do and think about, giving ourselves some time away from an unreasonable situation could reduce stress. If we move away physically but continue to think about the ways we feel offended, our stress level will increase. The cliché "time heals everything" sounds great, but I don't believe it's true.

We can avoid someone for years, but if during that time we've done nothing to address the inner anger we have toward that person, then no healing and no closure has taken place. Carrying around the baggage of unresolved conflicts reduces our ability to deal with present unreasonable situations.

## Stage Five: Reason Returns, Making Resolution Possible

When we give ourselves sufficient distance, reason normally return. This makes it possible for us to think logically and rationally. This gives us an opportunity to resolve our original issues. The first step in doing this is to examine the reasons for our anger—which are reflected in our conscious thoughts and root beliefs—and to determine whether or not they are based on truth and worth hanging on to.

For example, this morning I felt very angry with myself because I realized that I've missed the last two deadlines that I set for submitting this manuscript to my publisher. These were my conscious but unstated thoughts:

- It's no use trying to make the next deadline.
- I will miss it just like I always do.
- I might as well quit writing.

Were these thoughts based on truth and worth hanging on to? No! While it's true that I missed the last two deadlines, it's not true that I always miss my deadlines. I've consistently posted on my blog for 64 weeks. Did I decide to quit writing? No! Instead, I did some thinking and problem-solving, so that I could discover the reasons that I'd missed my deadlines.

That meant asking questions such as these: Is my next deadline realistic? What specific steps do I need to take in order to meet that deadline? Do I need help with any of these steps? Where will I get that help? How much time will it take me to finish this book, and how much time each day will I need to spend working on it? After answering these questions and making the changes that I needed to make, I felt calm. My adrenaline level was lower. I felt hopeful instead of frustrated and discouraged.

Examining the root reasons for our anger takes time and it involves hard work, but when we avoid thinking about the reason(s) for our anger and take no steps to reduce our stress, our frustration increases. It can develop into deep resentment.

## Stage Six: We Avoid Resolution

This habit of avoidance does not result in conflict resolution. It prevents closure. Closure is needed because anger is a social issue. Our anger affects others not just ourselves. For example, I may lose my temper, shout at my husband, and then drop my anger. But unless I tell him so my husband will not know that I am no longer angry. Until I tell him that I'm no longer angry, he may feel uncomfortable and avoid me. There will be no closure.

Lack of closure often means that we have pushed our anger underground. But it's still controlling us and we may develop an anger addiction. Denial goes hand-in-hand with an anger addiction (as it does with all addiction). It's painful to break through that denial, yet doing so—becoming aware of the unhealthy choices that we are making—is the first step to freedom.

With God's help we can develop self-control and use the capacity for anger that he gave to us for constructive purposes. That's the topic of my next chapter.

# 10

# Choose Self-control and Become Productive

> *Every* person can master his or her own anger. . . . Any person can develop constructive ways of expressing anger while extinguishing destructive old patterns.
>
> —Neil Clark Warren[1]

Once we've gained the courage to become honest about our anger and discovered some of the unhealthy and destructive choices that we've been making, we have the opportunity to make changes. By evaluating our choices and determining (according to the principles of God's Word) which ones are life-giving and which ones are not, we can stop making the choices which we see are destructive. By relying on the wisdom and empowerment of the Holy Spirit, we can discover and make healthier choices. We can learn how to handle anger in ways that result in improved communication and closer relationships; this will reduce the intensity of our anger, so that we can express our feelings without injuring others or ourselves.

The <u>Development of Self-control</u> drawing (<u>Image 6, page 184, in the Appendix</u>) shows the healthy choices that are available to us when we recognize that we are angry.

We have two choices: (1) Follow the direction of the sin nature and continue to make destructive choices, or (2) Follow the direction of the

Holy Spirit and, using the energy of anger for constructive purposes, grow the emotion (fruit) of self-control.

## Stage One: An Unacceptable Situation

Unrealistic expectations of ourselves and others can make us frustrated. We can ignore the truth of human frailty, disregard the fact that we live on a planet subject to destruction, and overlook injustices in the world, but the inability to feel angry about injustices, suffering, the destruction caused by evil people, the relational conflicts rampant in our culture, and the destruction of the environment hinders our functioning and limits our usefulness in life.

Jesus became passionately angry at the self-centered and greedy religious leaders of his day who were ripping off the poor. Here is the story:

> Jesus went straight to the Temple and threw out everyone who had set up shop, buying and selling. He kicked over the tables of loan sharks and the stalls of dove merchants. He [Jesus] quoted this text:
> My house was designated a house of prayer;
> You have made it a hangout for thieves.
> Now there was room for the blind and crippled to get in. They came to Jesus and he healed them.
> —21:12–14 (MSG)

I'm not using this illustration to advocate destructive behavior but rather to re-emphasize the fact that anger can give us power to take action when we need to do so. If we expect life to be perfect—free of conflict, pain and injustice—we turn minor difficulties into catastrophes, and our anger quickly and unnecessarily escalates.

For example, after writing my last paragraph, I took a break from my computer to vacuum the floor in my office. While doing so, I recognized that I was experiencing a rush of adrenaline and realized that I was feeling angry. Why? Because my new vacuum cleaner was not working as well as I expected it to work! Thankfully, I recognized that my anger was unhelpful and that it was causing me unnecessary stress, so I calmed myself.

## Stage Two: Notice Signs of Stress

In the development of self-control, noticing our signs of stress is a positive step. Doing so gives us an opportunity to reduce stress, and reducing stress gives us the ability to think clearly, so that we can examine the reasons for our stress—our root beliefs. If we need help in order to discover what our root beliefs are, then we can ask God—who knows what we are thinking—to show us these beliefs.

David tells us this in one of his prayers. He says, "You know when I sit down or stand up. You know my thoughts even when I'm far away" (Psalm 139:2 NLT). Other people, as well as God, can help us with this. For example, when I told my husband that I was not going to push myself to meet my self-imposed deadline to submit this book to my publisher by January 31, he said,

> "That's a relief!"
> "Why?" I asked. "Do I get stressed when I push myself too hard?"
> "Yes!"

His "yes" prompted me to ask for more information, and he gladly informed me of signs of stress that I'd been ignoring.

If we want the fruit of self-control to develop in our lives, then we must pay attention to the signals of stress that our mind and body send to us—things such as fatigue, irritability, muscle pain, hunger, and confusion. For example, this morning, when I sat down at my computer to start writing, I set my timer for thirty minutes; I intended to get up and stretch when it went off. When it I went off, I ignored it because I simply did not want to stop writing; about fifteen minutes later, signals of muscle pain and fatigue told me that I needed to get up and move, so I gave myself a "Time-out."

## Stage Three: Take a "Time-Out"

By taking a "Time-Out" when we recognize signs of stress, we can calm ourselves. Being able to get away from a situation for at least a few minutes is ideal. But even if it's not possible to get away, there are things we can do to calm ourselves. These are some of the possibilities:

- Do some deep breathing.
- Stretch.
- Focus on something beautiful.
- Pray silently.

When I do deep breathing I silently speak words. When inhaling, I say "praise" and on exhaling, I say "God." By doing this, I divert my attention away from the frustrating problem and calm my mind as well as my body.

Some people calm themselves by walking or running, some listen to music, others focus on a beautiful picture or do some craft such as knitting. By choosing to do these kinds of things, we can calm ourselves enough to think clearly.

If we want to stop expressing our anger in destructive and dysfunctional ways, then we must begin by recognizing and admitting to our anger. This includes paying attention to signals of stress in our bodies and taking the steps necessary to calm ourselves. Then, with clear thinking, we can move on to stage four in the development of self-control.

## Stage Four: Make a Wise Assessment

Making a wise assessment includes discovering the root of our anger and discerning whether or not our anger is justified. The root of anger, like any other emotional experience, is our heart beliefs. So, the first step in resolving anger is to identify these beliefs. That's not always easy. I have to get in touch with my heart. It would be easier when I feel the adrenaline rush of anger in my body to simply and quickly express that anger. But my expression would probably be destructive and unjustified. "Be quick to listen, slow to speak and slow to anger; for the anger of man does not achieve the righteousness of God," said James (1:19–20 NASB), in his short New Testament letter.

To get in touch with my heart beliefs I must quiet myself and listen to my *self-talk*—the thoughts circulating around in my head. This takes practice as well as silence. I often do it in the morning when I wake up. This morning, for instance, I woke up with physical pain. I groaned inwardly and turned over in bed. Tuning in to my thoughts, I heard—"It isn't fair! I'll never be able to make it through the day."

Then other words came into my consciousness—words of Scripture: "His plans for you are good" (Jeremiah 29:11 NLT). That meant I had a choice to make. I could either believe that God's plans for me were good or I could believe the "It isn't fair!" and "I'll never be able to make it through the day" thoughts in my head. Instead of turning over in bed, I got up, dressed, had breakfast, and walked my usual two miles. My pain level decreased and I felt strengthened. This is an example of choosing grace and receiving God's empowerment. He strengthens us when we act in accordance to the truth he speaks.

It's important to remember that feelings flow out of thoughts, and thoughts flow out of our heart beliefs. Unless we change our beliefs regarding a situation in which we feel angry, we will not be able to let go of our anger. Self-control grows in our lives when we listen to the words that the Holy Spirit speaks (his words of truth are always based on and in agreement with Scripture) and act accordingly. God, who never expresses anger inappropriately, will give us wisdom in every situation so that we can express our anger in a constructive way.

Being unable to detect and/or resolve anger drains us of energy. Perhaps that's why the Apostle Paul said, "Do not let the sun go down while you are still angry" (Ephesians 4:26 NIV). Constructive expressions of anger, along with resolution of the conflict, need to take place as quickly as possible after we have calmed down.

## Stage Five: Communicate With Grace and Truth

How can we express our anger in a way that's not destructive? There are two basic elements: grace and truth. In our conversations, grace needs to be the larger component and truth the smaller component. In one of his letters to early Christians, Paul says, "Let your conversation be gracious and attractive so that you will have the right response for everyone" (Colossians 4:6 NLT).

Paul made this statement in the context of sharing the message of the Gospel, but I think the principle is applicable when we are attempting to express anger in a healthy and constructive way. Our desire to be right and disclose everything we feel needs to be less important than our desire to restore relationships.

We can learn to ask the Holy Spirit to help us control our tongue. I recently needed this help when I was listening to a teaching I disagreed with. I wanted to blurt out, "You are wrong!" but I knew it would not accomplish anything good. "A fool always loses his temper, but a wise man holds it back" (Proverbs 29:11 NASB) is a proverb worth memorizing.

The Holy Spirit showed me that expressing my anger (in that situation) would not accomplish his purposes. I like the way Eugene Peterson phrases this truth in his paraphrase of Scripture: "Post this at all the intersections, dear friends: Lead with your ears, follow up with your tongue, and let anger straggle along in the rear. God's righteousness doesn't grow from human anger" (James 1:19–20 MSG).

Disagreeing with a teacher's message when I was a visitor in the church would have been very disrespectful. Challenging this teacher would have been disrespectful to him, and it would have caused unnecessary conflict within his congregation. It would have been like a stranger invading and challenging the beliefs and behavior of a family gathering. I could have left the situation, but, in addition to disrupting the group, I would not have been able to visit with my friends. So I stayed and silently prayed. The Holy Spirit gave me grace to control my tongue. Later, when my blood pressure and heartbeat had returned to normal, so that I could think more clearly, I discussed the situation with my husband.

How can we make a wise assessment when we believe something is unreasonable? Often it helps to talk with someone who is neutral—a friend, a counselor or a pastor. Through prayer, we can ask God to show us his perspective of this situation. We may discover our anger is inappropriate or out of proportion to the situation and choose to drop it. Or we may find that our anger is appropriate; then we can express it in a constructive way.

## Step Six: Take Appropriate Action

In order to develop self-control, we must take the action that's necessary to accept or resolve the unreasonable situation. Accepting a situation doesn't mean we like the situation; it means that we do what we can to find inner peace, and that might mean leaving a situation rather than remaining in it. We can become stuck by staying in a situation that we believe is unreasonable. We can become stuck by staying with a person whom we believe is unreasonable. And we can become stuck by staying glued to our own unreasonable thinking.

We don't have power to change the beliefs or behavior of others. We only have power to change our own beliefs and behavior. If the unreasonable behavior and attitudes of others does not change, and our unreasonable situation does not improve, must we remain angry? Only if we cling to the untrue, irrational, and negative, beliefs in our heads!

If we know that our thinking determines our behavior and that errors in our thinking are the root cause of our anger, then why wouldn't we want to change our thinking? There are two possibilities: (1) We aren't aware of our untrue, irrational or negative thoughts. (2) We don't know of any true, rational, or positive thoughts to replace them with.

How can we detect errors in our thinking? (1) By reflective thinking, we can sometimes discover them ourselves. (2) By asking us pertinent questions, a counselor might be able to help us detect them. (3) Most importantly, we can ask God, who knows everything, to reveal our heart beliefs to us. That's usually a starting point in the process of change. (Some people in my classes have discovered their heart beliefs by practicing the discipline of prayer-journaling that I described in Chapter Eight.)

We might resist changing because we enjoy the feeling of power that anger gives to us. We like the adrenalin rush that we feel when we get angry. The question we need to ask ourselves is this: "Do I want my anger to control me or do I want to control my anger?" Thinking goes on vacation and our brains becomes useless when we allow anger to control us. Uncontrolled anger depletes us of the energy we need to solve problems.

God calls us to do all we can to resolve unreasonable situations. Through Paul, he encourages us to "Do all that [we] can to live in peace with everyone" (Romans 12:18 NLT).

## Stage Seven: Face Future Situations Free of "Baggage"

Doing the work it takes to accept or resolve an unreasonable situation frees us to address upcoming anger-producing situations with energy and hope. We face future situations free of "baggage." This gives us confidence and hope that we can resolve future problems.

In the following lines from her prayer-journal, Donna tells how she's learning to express anger in a constructive way, resolving issues rather than avoiding them.

> Jesus, I am nowhere near as bad as I used to be with anger. Of course I am older and have fewer hormones driving me. My living situation is much better, and I am more mature. Another factor is: I am closer to you and count on you more than I ever did before. I do know, like Jane, I have disturbed sleep if I go through the night angry. When I don't resolve the problem, but I just take all the blame, apologize and go on from there, the issue is still there. I know better now, and I don't do that with . . . . Through Jane's class I have learned I can control my anger and manage my time . . . I am a happier person.

Ignored and unaddressed anger can become addictive, and it can, also, develop into resentment and revenge. *Resentment*, or frozen anger, can hide like an iceberg beneath the surface of our consciousness. In the next chapter, I provide clues for recognizing resentment.

# 11

# Uncover Bitter Resentment

> Resentment, or 'frozen anger,' is probably the prime killer of emotional health . . . [It] kills creativity in the soul and destroys any incentive to recover from addiction.
>
> —James Houston[1]

A few years ago, after we'd moved to a new location, my husband and I planted a vegetable garden. Gardening was not new for us, and the gardens we'd planted in past years yielded an abundance of vegetables, so, feeling confident about our gardening skills and eager to eat fresh produce, we purchased and planted our favorite seeds. They sprouted and began to grow. We watered them and removed the weeds. The plants took root and grew taller. We couldn't wait to eat the snow peas, green beans, and tomatoes that we'd planted. You can imagine how surprised and dismayed we felt when we walked into our garden one sunny day and saw all the plants wilting. "What's happening?" we asked one another. "Is some insect eating them? Are they diseased?"

We examined them for both of these possibilities but found no evidence of either disease or destruction by insects. Our plants kept on wilting, then they turned yellow, and soon they died. One of our friends discovered the cause of their death. It was the huge Black walnut tree which stood in our back yard. The tree was beautiful; it provided us with shade and looked attractive, but its roots contained a poisonous substance which spread through the soil and killed off all of our vegetable plants.

Resentment is like the poisonous root of a black walnut tree. When we allow this root to grow in our hearts, it exhausts us, robs of us joy, and produces the fruit of bitterness. Like the roots of a black walnut tree, resentment does its nasty work underground. We may not intentionally plant and cultivate it, and we may be unaware of its presence. We can see signs of it in others, yet remain blind to the resentment hidden in our own hearts. If we *do* recognize resentment in ourselves, we may not understand how it developed, and we don't know how to get rid of it.

The Map of Resentment drawing (Image 7, page 185, in the Appendix) shows how resentment develops and is maintained.

## Stage One: Frustration Accumulates Over Time

Frustration can accumulate because of small, everyday problems. For example, I feel frustrated about my physical limitations almost every day. I'm thankful for my hearing aids, but they certainly are not like having new ears. I get annoyed and impatient tying to adjust them in various settings. Sometimes, I feel frustrated about the chronic pain I have, and I find it hard to accept the fact of decreased energy.

Frustration can also accumulate because of larger issues. A few years ago, during the sudden and unexpected death of a close friend, God brought me face to face with the resentment I'd hidden in my heart. It had developed into an emotional addiction in which I felt stuck and did very little with my gifting. The root of my resentment was anger toward God for taking away—for the second time—a close friend and true supporter.

Frustration can result from many factors. The following is a non-exclusive list:

- An inability to solve problems
- Unresolved and buried anger
- Lack of direction or leadership
- Unclear goals and purposes
- Difficult circumstances (such as a job loss or illness) over which we have no control
- Unreasonable expectations of ourselves or others (such as perfection)
- Unaccepted losses
- Feeling a lack of support and understanding
- Confusion about identity and/or role
- Unfulfilled needs and desires.

We are imperfect people who live in an imperfect world with other imperfect people; we could feel disappointed, hurt and frustrated almost every day, but frustration doesn't have to develop. It depends on what we choose to believe and do.

## Stage Two: We Believe Lies about God, Self, and Others

As I explained in chapter three, the root of any emotion is our heart beliefs. When my friend died, I believed (1) that God did not have my best interest in mind; (2) He was unfair to take her away; and (3) I couldn't live without her support. These beliefs composed the root from which my resentment grew.

Sometimes we forget what the original frustrating issue was, but, like a hidden sliver, it festers and grows in our unconscious mind. I was unaware of my hidden resentment—fueled by lies about God, others, and myself—for nearly seven years until, upon the death of my second friend, God graciously revealed them to me.

In his book *The Lies We Believe,* Dr. Chris Thurman talks about common lies people believe. The following lies that could keep us trapped in resentment:

- "I Must Be Perfect"
- "I Must Have Everyone's Love And Approval"
- "I Can't Be Happy Unless Things Go My Way"
- "It's Somebody Else's Fault"
- "Life Should Be Fair"
- "You Can And Should Meet All My Needs"
- "It Is My Christian Duty To Meet The Needs Of Others"
- "A Good Christian Doesn't Feel Angry, Anxious Or Depressed"[2]

## Stage Three: We Distrust and Blame God, Self, and/or Others

For years I distrusted God because I believed he had favorites, and I thought that I was not one of them. This angered me because without his favor I did not expect to succeed in life. I read in Scripture that his plans for me were good, but in my heart I believed this statement applied to someone else—not me. Recently, the Holy Spirit revealed the truth of Scripture to my heart so that I could see myself as someone who could expect good things from God. This is the Scripture that I read: "There will be trouble and distress for every human being who does evil: first for the Jew, then for the Gentile; but glory, honor and peace for everyone who does good: first for the Jew, then for the Gentile. For God does not show favoritism" (Romans 2:9–11 NIV).

I realized that I am a person who does good—not perfectly, but patiently. So, God *will* reward me. I can trust him. He does not have favorites. He is fair. Trust grows when we focus on God and who he is, rather than on how we feel or on what may be happening in our situation. When Abraham was ninety years old, God told him that he would have a child. Abraham believed God, not because of the evidence in his body but because of his confidence that God would keep his promise. When my body feels weak and I continue to have symptoms of digestive issues, I don't despair. I live in the strength that the Lord provides.

## Stage Four: We Bury our Feelings and Live in Denial

If I, as a Christian, believe a good Christian doesn't feel angry, anxious or depressed, then I will certainly not tell anyone I possess those feelings, and I will probably hide them from myself. For many years, that's what I did with my anger, anxiety, and depression. Honestly confessing my distrust and anger toward God regarding my friend's death shortly after it occurred would have freed me and kept me from building resentment. Instead I buried my thoughts and feelings.

How often we Christian people fail to acknowledge the struggles we have with these feelings when a loved one dies! Maybe we think it will spoil our testimony if we show negative emotions at such a time. What may be more noticeable is our lack of transparency. When we bury our feelings, pretend to ourselves (and others) that everything is fine, smile, and act as if we are perfectly happy, we are being emotionally dishonest.

This, in her words, is what Stephanie discovered about emotional honesty and effective communication:

> I sometimes pretend that things are okay, and then I find that I resent the person for believing me. I now realize that this behavior is dysfunctional since I am not being honest with myself or the other person. As a wife and mom of three children, I am often

asked what I would like for everyone to do regarding chores, grocery shopping, how to spend the day. Before learning the concepts in Jane's book, I would always low-ball my needs. That is, if I wanted both of our bathrooms in our house to be cleaned, the trash taken out and the laundry folded, I would only communicate that I wanted the trash taken out. Then later on, when I would be feeling frustrated that the other things were not done —no fault of my family—I would then angrily tell them that I wanted those things done. This behavior was neither open nor honest communication. I need to be honest with others and myself so that I do not set myself up for emotionally destructive patterns of behavior.

Polite smiles and rationalizations can serve to camouflage resentment, but buried frustrations keep us stuck in the past.

## Stage Five: We Feel Stuck

We feel stuck, not because of the situation we are in but because of the hidden beliefs (often lies) we have about that situation. When I moved away from my writing group and my supportive friends died, I got stuck in a "writing block." This wasn't because of my situation. It was because of the beliefs I had about that situation such as "I can't write without their support" and "God isn't fair."

Maintaining an unforgiving spirit will also keep us stuck. Hanging on to lies and grudges, even though I was unaware of them, kept me from making significant progress in the area of writing. While walking with my husband this morning, I prayed that God would show me any hidden resentment. The Holy Spirit brought to my conscious mind an incident that occurred over twenty years ago over which I still held resentment. I acknowledged and confessed my resentment and shared the incident with my husband. As we talked about it, I saw the past situation from a fresh point-of-view, forgave my husband, and let go of the grudge.

Hanging on to grudges and refusing to forgive keeps us from remembering and enjoying the positive aspects of past situations. When we continue to focus on past hurts (mentally rehearsing them), we continue to experience pain. This inner pain can cause us to become impatient and snappy toward others. We may smile on the outside but indirectly lash out.

## Stage Six: We Indirectly Lash Out

One way buried frustrations surface is through indirect lashing out. Lashing out temporarily relieves frustration, but it does not resolve the underlying problems. We might indirectly lash out at God by holding a grudge against him and/or avoiding prayer and Bible study. We might lash out toward others through sarcasm, joking, and gossip. We also might silently lash out by avoiding one another or by silence (refusing to communicate). Lack of communication produces confusion and increases frustration.

If we are perfectionists with high expectations for ourselves, we might hold a grudge against ourselves for past mistakes and failures and lash out toward ourselves. How do we know whether or not we are holding a grudge against ourselves (or others)? One indication is our self-talk— the silent comments we speak to ourselves throughout the day. Our feelings about an event are created by these messages. If we are constantly putting ourselves down or scolding ourselves—in our minds or with our mouth—then we probably resent ourselves.

I often become impatient with myself, disappointed when I do not accomplish everything on my list for the day. In the evening, I might look at my list and rebuke myself with messages such as these:

"Couldn't you have done better? Is that all you've accomplished?" A few months ago, I found a website offering brain-games. "Great!" I said, "This will be fun!" After a few months, however, doing the games became more frustrating than fun. Why? I could not handle a decrease in my performance. A goal of expecting constant improvement increases frustration in my life.

Other ways that we might lash out at ourselves include keeping negative self-talk going and being intentionally incompetent—purposely performing below the level of our ability by procrastinating and partially or poorly finishing projects.

One area of accumulated frustration for me is the collection of boxes, full of unsorted items, setting in my basement and in my closets—stuff I've accumulated for forty years and dragged from one house to another in various moves. Often, I've taken a box from the shelf, started looking thought it, and then stuffed everything back in and returned it to the shelf. I haven't been able to figure out why I've made such little progress on this project. I've felt stuck.

## Stage Seven: We Feel and Act Like a Victim

One day, as I prayed and reflected on my house full of unsorted boxes, I realized that I had hidden resentment about moving. I wrote a list of frustrations that I had experienced in my various moves and discovered that I felt like a victim. I had hidden resentment toward my husband for losses and hurts I'd experienced, and I was blaming *him* for some of my choices. If I believe I can't be happy unless someone else changes, then I will be stuck in my unhappiness. Blaming my husband kept me from seeing the choices that I had made, including a failure to communicate my desires.

Having a victim mentality includes blaming others for our problems; when we blame others, we lose a sense of responsibility for our choices, and we feel helpless and powerless. Feelings of helplessness and powerlessness promote self-pity. Self-pity has the opposite effect of true comfort; instead of reducing the pain of a situation, it magnifies that pain.

John Piper calls self-pity "the voice of pride in the heart of the weak."[3] It's a way of saying we deserve recognition for our suffering. Self-pity goes hand in hand with a lack of trust; it prevents us from seeking help either from God or others. God will give us the answers we need if we come to him in humble faith. He generously gives wisdom to all who ask. (James 1:2–8)

## Stage Eight: We Become a Prisoner of Bitterness

Nourishing a victim mentality makes us unproductive and unhappy: we neglect working on our problems, our frustration accumulates, and we become envious and critical of others.

The following poem (written by a friend of mine and used with his permission) illustrates the tragic consequence for someone who chose bitterness throughout his life.

> My dad went to church when he was a boy.
> An evangelist told a story about another boy who had a little pet snake.
> He fed it mice and frogs; it ate, and ate, and grew, and grew—
> 'Till one day it wrapped itself around the boy's neck and squeezed
> 'Till the boy died, and his head turned blue.
>
> "Sin is like that snake!" the evangelist said,
> "And if you don't repent, it will strangle you, and you too, will be dead."

My dad had nightmares for a long while after that.
   First, anger and dread,
*Then bitterness against church settled in.*
When he grew up he didn't care to go back there
   again.

At the age of eight he left the farm and went to stay
   with his newly married sister in another place,
'Cause his dad was sick, or maybe because my dad
   was fifteen years younger than sis and the folks
   needed some space.
He didn't complain, but he sure wanted to go back
   home again.
*And each night he took bitterness to bed with him.*

Well, in a couple of years he moved back with Mom
   and Dad.
In high school, he knew more than his teachers, or
   so he thought.
The physics teacher tried to flunk him; dad outsmarted
   the guy and got his A.
*But he had bitterness against schools and teachers, after
   that day.*

Dad dropped out of college and eloped with his high
   school sweetheart.
It was 1928 and no one knew the depression was ready
   to start.
The marriage wasn't what he expected. He was used
   to having a blast;
But a baby came, the stock market crashed, and life
   got real hard real fast.
*Bitterness was the only feeling he could amass.*

> The only job he could get was on the steel mill
> electrical crew.
> The bosses were cruel and if you complained you
> were through.
> He said it was like prison, except you went home at
> night—one big black hole.
> *It was the only way to get a paycheck; and he put a lot more
> bitterness in his soul.*
>
> At seventy-eight they took him to the hospital because
> he couldn't move.
> My sister was there when he was ready to die.
> *She said, "He just laid there with a glare of bitterness in
> his eye."*
>
> The death certificate said, "Cause of death: a stroke."
> But I knew that was a joke.
> *My dad was slowly strangled by a snake called bitterness.*

If we feed the "snake called bitterness" its poison will deaden our emotions and paralyze our spirits. Eventually, like the man described in the above poem, we will be unable to make any other choice.

Thankfully, through the wisdom, grace, and power that God provides, we can learn to make different choices and experience joy instead of bitterness. I describe those choices in the next chapter.

# 12

# Embrace Truth and Discover Joy

> Always be joyful. Never stop praying. Be thankful in all circumstances, for this is God's will for you who belong to Christ Jesus.
> —1 Thessalonians 5: 16–18 (NLT)

I hesitated to use the above Scripture in my introduction to this chapter because many times it's been wrongly applied. It's been used as a verbal whip by Christians who lack empathy to "shape-up" wounded fellow believers, as a bumper-sticker phrase to advertise our faith, or as a simple and quick way to get rid of sad feelings.

Does this instruction, which Paul gave to the early Christian church, apply to us today? Are we still expected to live according to the absolute standard of expressing gratitude in *all* circumstances? Giving thanks in *every* painful and difficult situation? Yes, I believe God still expects this. It *is* reasonable. It *is* possible. What makes it seem unreasonable and impossible is: (1) a misunderstanding of what this instruction says and means and (2) a lack of understanding on how to get there. I hope my explanation and illustrations will help you understand what it means to "be thankful in all circumstances" and give you helpful guidelines for doing so.

The Development of Joy drawing (Image 8, page 186, in the Appendix) shows choices that help us avoid resentment, grow in faith and gratitude, and maintain joy and productivity in the midst of frustrating circumstances.

## Stage One: Expect Frustration in Life

Recently, a dear woman in our church stood up and shared how God was working in her life to give her joy. "When I became a Christian, I expected that everything would be easy," she said. "God would answer my prayers immediately; instead he is taking me through the frustrations."

Sometimes, we Christians paint a false picture of what life will be like for others when they trust Christ and begin to live according to his directions. We promise them a pain-free, problem-free, and conflict-free existence. This is not what Jesus promised. He told us that as long as we are on this earth we would have "trials and sorrows" (John 16:33 NLT).

Rose has been experiencing the truth of Jesus' statement. It's been a difficult few weeks. Her husband, after being unable to find work for several months, finally found a job, but it was located hundreds of miles away—much too far for him to commute on a daily or even a weekly basis. She's been alone with their three small children. Since it looked like they would be moving, she started packing boxes. In the midst of this, her three children became sick with the flu. Finally she was summoned to come to the hospital because her father was dying of cancer. Despite these circumstances, she came to church on Sunday morning. When she stepped out of her van, she smiled and thanked me for my prayers. I was amazed by her joy!

Rose is not a fake. She's genuine. She doesn't pretend that things have been easy. She doesn't thank God *for* her husband's job commute, loss, flu, and cancer. But, in the midst of these difficult circumstances, she *is* thankful. She's following Paul's instruction: "Be thankful *in* all things."

His instruction is not: Be thankful *for* all things. I do not give thanks for muscle pain, sleepless nights, and the death of friends. I do give thanks *in* these circumstances because, by the strength and grace God gives to me, I do not feel overwhelmed.

Rose also knows—in her frustrating circumstances—where to receive help, and she's humble enough to recognize that she needs support, and she asks for it.

## Stage Two: Share Frustration with God and/or a Trusted Friend

When I speak about sharing our frustrations, I do not mean we should dump, complain, and gossip. That kind of behavior might feel good for the moment, but it is only a temporary fix. There's only one thing that changes when we dump on others: the people to whom we complain get tired of hearing us and we have to find someone else to complain to.

We probably all know people who constantly gripe about their frustrations in life and gossip about others. They don't understand why people are unfriendly. Listening to them makes us feel very weary. They are stuck in the cycle of addictive resentment. The opposite end of the spectrum is faking it—denying that we feel discouraged and frustrated. Growing up in a family in which people did not talk about feelings, I practiced denial for years. Gradually, I learned how to appropriately share my pain and frustration. When we share our frustrations for the purpose of seeking insight and wisdom so that we can change, then our sharing is useful.

I am deeply thankful for the many helpful and supportive persons and resources God has provided for me over the years—faithful friends, an understanding husband, wise counselors, authors of books, composers of songs, and—most importantly—God himself. All of us become discouraged and frustrated when we withdraw and live in isolation. Our perspective is limited. Sharing with others expands our horizon so that we can see past clouds of pain and confusion.

## Stage Three: Embrace Truth and Gain a Faith-Perspective

We can learn how to overcome resentment by looking at the stories of faith displayed by Old Testament characters. Hannah serves as an excellent example of someone whose bitterness dissolved when she gained a faith-perspective. Her story is recorded in the first and second chapters of 1 Samuel.

Hannah was childless. Her husband, Elkanah, was a polygamist—a culturally acceptable practice at that time. His other wife, Peninnah, had several children. Peninnah constantly reminded Hannah of her of childlessness, teasing and provoking her. How could any woman live under these circumstances without becoming bitter? Hannah felt extremely upset—so upset, that at times, she could not eat.

Finally, when her husband took her along on his yearly visit to the tabernacle, Hannah poured out her pain to God. She was so distressed that a priest who saw her weeping accused her of being drunk. She replied, "I haven't been drinking wine or anything stronger. But I am very discouraged, and I was pouring out my heart to the LORD. Don't think I am a wicked woman! For I have been praying out of great anguish and sorrow" (1 Samuel 1:15–16 NLT).

*Jane Ault*

The priest accepted this explanation, prayed that God would give Hannah a child, and gave her a blessing of peace. Hannah embraced truth and gained a faith perspective.

- She believed that God cared for her.
- She realized that he was not condemning her for sharing feelings of bitterness.
- She knew that he'd seen the pain and injustice under which she was living.
- She was confident that he would give her the desire of her heart.

Because of these new beliefs, Hannah had hope. She felt comforted. She received grace to go back home to the same situation, and (I assume) she was able to handle it. When we choose to trust God and/or another friend, being open about our feelings, we usually gain the perspective of faith—"confidence that what we hope for will actually happen" (Hebrews 11:1 NLT).

Though we may see no solution for our problems, God does, and he calls us to place our hope in him. When we place our hope in him, we no longer need to cling to the grudges we have held against others or to the expectations that we've placed upon them.

## Stage Four: Let Go of Grudges and Expectations

Since Hannah was as human as we are, she may well have held a grudge against Peninnah for the meanness handed down to her over the years. What did the relationship between these two women look like after Hannah returned from her visit to the temple? The Bible doesn't tell us. But it does say that Hannah was no longer sad and that she began to eat. This indicates that she felt loved. I believe that hope, faith, and the comfort she received from Gold gave her strength to let go of any grudges she was carrying.

Knowing that we are loved gives us the courage to let go of our bitterness. During the month I wrote this chapter, I decided to focus on the topic of love. One of my goals was to memorize the 13th chapter of the book of First Corinthians—a beautiful description of love. Among the characteristics of love that are listed is this one: "It [love] is not irritable or resentful." I read that Scripture several times before I understood that in love there is no resentment—none at all. How would I feel if I did not carry any resentment in life? No resentment either toward myself or others? I would be free of a great weight. I would have energy to spare. Deeply desiring this freedom, I started to cry.

Then, as I continued searching the Scripture, I found these other two statements: "The love of Christ controls us" (2 Corinthians 5:14 NCV) and "God was reconciling the world to himself in Christ, not counting people's sins against them" (2 Corinthians 5:19 NIV). All of my life I've resisted the idea of being controlled by anything or anybody; yet, resentment has controlled many of my days. It *does* count people's sins against them.

Being controlled by resentment is slavery. Being controlled by love is freedom. Being controlled by love happens when we submit our hearts and lives to God. This involves trust. For Ann Voskamp, developing a lifestyle of gratitude produced an unexpected benefit—increased trust in God. She says: *"Count blessings and discover Who can be counted on. . . .* Trust is the bridge from yesterday to tomorrow, built with planks of thanks. Remembering frames up gratitude. Gratitude lays out the planks of trust. I can walk the planks—from known to unknown—and know: He holds."[1]

What we remember about any given situation is a matter of choice. If we believe God loves us and that he is able to bring good out of every situation (the promise of Romans 8:28), we will trust him and experience joy. But if, in our minds, we choose to remember and think about pain and hardships, we will prolong our bondage to resentment.

About a year ago, I was scheduled to have cataract surgery. When I went for my pre-op appointment and saw a video describing the procedures (including possible complications) I panicked and cancelled my surgery. What caused me to make that decision? I remembered a what-was-supposed-to-be ambulatory surgery nine months earlier in which I experienced unusual complications.

These are the things about that situation that I choose to remember: my physician's diagnostic failure, hospitalization that lasted for almost three weeks, unexpected and unnecessary physical pain, a medication overdose, a three hour ambulance transfer to another hospital, a corrective surgery, and very long recovery.

## Stage Five: Give Thanks, Have Renewed Energy and Joy

These are the things about my complicated surgery that I chose to forget: the loving care I received from my husband and church family, the fact that someone did eventually make a correct diagnosis, the kindness of hospital staff and ambulance drivers, the expertise of surgeons in the larger hospital, the miraculous way in which God brought me out of the medication overdose, the prayers, cards, phone calls and visits from family and friends, the fact that we had good insurance coverage and did not end up in bankruptcy.

As these events were taking place, I felt God's presence and grace. I expressed gratitude. I felt great joy to be alive. Unfortunately, over the ensuing months, I forgot the blessings and focused on the hardships and pain, perpetuating resentment and fear and needlessly cancelling my cataract surgery.

We can choose to remember pain and hardships and experience anger, pain and sorrow, or we can choose to recall blessings and answers to prayer and experience joy. Resentment exhausts us but joy energizes us. The Old Testament prophet Nehemiah told a congregation of depressed and weeping people to celebrate, for "the joy of the Lord" (Nehemiah 8:10 NIV) was their strength.

Joy-of-the-Lord-strength is directly connected to an understanding of our identity and gifting. Jesus modeled that strength. While on a road trip with his disciples, he struck up a conversation with a spiritually hungry woman whom he met at wayside well. Not wanting to linger, his disciples left and went into a nearby town in search of food. Jesus found his conversation with the woman so fulfilling that he was physically energized by it. When his disciples returned and offered him food, he said, "My nourishment comes from doing the will of God, who sent me, and from finishing his work" (John 4:34 NLT).

When we discover the reason for our existence—the purpose and destiny God has for us—and commit ourselves to doing his will we find great joy. Our hearts will be filled with gratitude. We will be able to give thanks in all circumstances because we've experienced God's love, we are confident of his goodness, and we know that by his power within in us we can overcome any obstacle. Gratitude will be our natural response.

## Stage Six: Develop a Lifestyle of Gratitude

My husband has developed a lifestyle of gratitude. He is constantly saying "Thank you"—thank you to God, thank you to me, and thank you to others. Throughout the day and in the night, I hear him say "Thank you." At times I've felt irritated by his thankfulness. That's because I felt convicted by it, knowing that my heart was full of complaints. I've been working to change that. And it *is* work. I know I can't do it on my own. I know I can't do it without God's empowering grace. Knowing that he is a forgiving God, slow to anger, kind, gentle and eager to give me wisdom and instruction, encourages me to persevere in my journey.

In Ann Voskamp's book, *One Thousand Gifts,* she shares her transforming experience of developing a life-style of gratitude. In discovering the relationship between gratitude and joy she says, "While I may not always feel joy, God asks me to give thanks in all things, because He knows that the *feeling* of joy begins in the *action* of thanksgiving . . . Joy is God and God is joy and joy doesn't negate all other emotions—joy *transcends* all other emotions."[2]

## Stage Seven: Resolve or Accept Frustration, Daily

A man from my church recently returned from a trip to a third world country. One of the things that surprised him was the amount of garbage strewn all over the land. "I was shocked," he said, "when at a picnic I attended everyone, when they were through eating, just tossed their plates into the air behind them. What used to be beautiful beaches now looked like unsanitary landfills!" When he brought up the possibility of cleaning the place up, people laughed at him and said, "That's the way it is here."

If we ignore daily frustrations, our inner hearts will eventually become smelly landfills filled with so much bitterness that the cleanup job can feel overwhelming. If, however, we deal with our frustrations on a daily basis, our task becomes manageable—though if we have a landfill to start with, we may need some time to clear out the clutter.

To reduce my daily load of frustrations, I'm working on these simple changes:

- Making a shorter to-do list—adjusted to the reality of my limitations, along with my understanding of God's purpose for me
- Thanking God at the end of the day for what, by his strength, I accomplished—instead of complaining about what I failed to accomplish

- Reminding myself that frustration is a normal part of life
- Monitoring my level of joy throughout the day.

I monitor my joy level by noting how often I sing. When I am happy, I spontaneously sing. Resentment blocks my song. Another helpful habit is paying attention to my energy level. Resentment drains me of energy. Recognizing and accepting my need for sleep—and readjusting my expectation for the day when I oversleep—reduces frustration.

Talking about the importance of sleep, Dr. Richard Swenson says, "Most people do best with seven to eight hours of sleep per night. Some need more — Einstein famously got ten to twelve hours per night and did not feel the need to apologize. . . Everything we do, we do better rested. The rested, stimulated brain thinks creative and productive thoughts. The exhausted brain thinks only of sleep."[3] When I'm rested, my perspective is more positive. I'm more thankful than when I'm exhausted. When I'm rested I have more energy.

## Stage Eight: Experience Continued Joy and Creative Productivity

Resentment drains us of energy, takes away our joy, and reduces our productivity. Yet because it's addictive, we often continue choosing it. In discovering and fulfilling God's purpose for us, we find immense strength and immeasurable joy. This joy stimulates our creativity, but it's not addictive. Why not? Because of the following choices:

- We express gratitude to God (and others).
- We rely on his grace.
- We practice forgiveness.
- We find fulfillment by pursing our calling.

Recently, I visited a friend who has a two-month old infant. As I held him in my arms and rocked back-and-forth in a glider, I could feel his body relax and see the wrinkles on his brow disappear. He was content. A heart full of gratitude (a thankful heart) is an antidote to addiction because it's a heart of *contentment*—satisfied with what it has.

Relying on God's grace is an antidote to the addictive passions of the sin nature because it's a dependence based on reality. We truly need grace. It offers us both forgiveness and empowerment. It teaches us to deny addictive passions and grow in the fruit of self-control. Practicing forgiveness frees us from heavy loads of frustration, judgment and guilt that rob us of the energy we need to pursue our calling. It also frees up our imagination which, when we entertain unforgiveness, remains focused on past wounds.

It's easy to understand how people with deep hurts could choose the pathway of bitterness; but anyone, facing the small annoyances of daily life, can become a "wound-collector." We must "keep a sharp eye out for weeds of bitter discontent. A thistle or two gone to seed can ruin a whole garden in no time" (Hebrews 12:15 MSG). In the following incident, I could have easily allowed resentment to develop.

While celebrating our forty-eighth wedding anniversary, John and I spent two days at a beautiful little cottage in Maine. On our departure, John grabbed several plastic bags of what-he-assumed was garbage and tossed them in the recycling bin. About forty-five minutes later, I realized that John's thermal cup—the one with photos of our grandchildren—was missing. This was our following conversation:

> "John, how many plastic bags did you throw into the recycling bin?"
> "I don't know. I just picked up all of the bags and threw them in."
> "Did you look to see what was in them?"

"No!"

"Well, I wish you had! Some of those bags did *not* contain garbage, and I think that your thermal cup was in one of them!"

Neither one of us could remember when we had last seen John's cup; so after searching the car and not finding it, we turned around and drove back to the cottage. Just as we drove into the recycling area, John said, "I think that I may have placed that cup on the floor of the back seat and it could have rolled underneath my seat." He got out of the car, reached under the front seat and pulled out his thermos. What was our response? We both laughed!

Forty-eight years ago, neither one of us would responded to such an event with laughter. I would have reacted in anger and added another item to the grudge-collection stored in my heart. How thankful I am for the emotional maturity that by God's grace both my husband and I have worked into our lives!

Why would any of us want to cling to resentment, when we could experience freedom and joy? Despite its consequences, many of us cling to bitterness. God allows us to make this choice, but it makes us vulnerable to revenge, the destructive emotion that I will discuss in chapter 13.

# 13

## Admit to Stubborn Revenge

Do not say, "I'll do to them as they have done to me;
I'll pay them back for what they did."
— Proverbs 24:29 (NIV)

A relative of mine told me the following story about a dog her family owned. This dog was very protective of his boundaries. He got offended if a stranger walked through their doorway, and more than once he bit someone. One day her pastor paid a visit. My relative, wondering how the dog would act, felt a bit anxious; but when the pastor arrived the dog did not seem to be disturbed. He did not even growl. He just sat quietly watching while the pastor sat down and visited for about an hour. But when the pastor got up to leave, the dog, without warning, lunged at him and fastened his teeth in the man's leg.

Revengeful people act like that dog. Their attacks are as unpredictable as the weather. Like a tornado in the middle of the night, they bring destruction. When we carry long-term resentment in our hearts we can become revengeful. Even if we not aware of a vengeful spirit in our hearts, it will destroy both our relationships and our health.

By learning what the stages and signs of revenge are and asking God to show us our hearts, we can discover whether or not we are revengeful. The <u>Map of Revenge</u> drawing <u>(Image 9, page 187, in the Appendix)</u> shows how revenge develops.

## Stage One: We Suffer a Violation/Loss

My relative's dog was protecting a boundary, the threshold of his owner's house. When the pastor who was a stranger stepped over it, the dog punished him for breaking a rule. Every person, family, and society has a set of rules, or boundaries, which they live by— rules concerning property, communication, space, feelings, responsibilities, etc. When our rules are not respected we feel violated—hurt, offended, disrespected, or dishonored.

Unfortunately, we don't always tell others what our rules are. We expect our friends and family to know what we're thinking and wanting. When they don't figure it out, we feel offended. How can we hold someone responsible for offending or hurting us when we fail to tell them what we want and expect?

For example, when my husband and I first got married, I wanted to please him so I did not tell him what I wanted. He would ask me what restaurant that I wanted to go to. I would think about where *he* might like to go; then, I'd tell him that's where I wanted to go. Afterwards, I felt resentful because he did not choose the restaurant I wanted to go. I thought loving others meant pleasing them at all times. I misinterpreted Jesus' commandment to love my neighbor as myself. I interpreted that commandment to mean "love your neighbor instead of yourself". That heart belief kept me from telling others what I wanted.

I did not grow up with a clear understanding of boundaries. Through reading Henry Cloud and John Townsend's book, *Boundaries*, working through their video series, and teaching it numerous times, I've gained a clear understanding of boundaries, and I'm learning to manage my boundaries more successfully. "Boundaries define us [they explain]. They define *what is me and what is not me*. A boundary shows me where I end and someone else begins, leading me to a sense of ownership."[1]

Our skin is our physical boundary. Everything inside our skin belongs to us: heart, lungs, muscles, glands, etc. God gave us the responsibility to care of our physical body and protect it. Sexual abuse and physical abuse are violations of that boundary.

Our will is another boundary. God gave us the ability and freedom to make choices, and he holds us responsible for the choices we make. Manipulating and controlling the choices of others violates their boundaries. We object when someone tries to take over and/or control something that belongs to us such as our money, our time, our talents, and our decisions—how we use these things. We value freedom of choice, and the right we have to protect what we own. If that right is taken away we feel violated.

As I write this, there's a conflict going on over the issue of gun control in our country. Many gun owners believe that the government's restrictions on gun purchasing and ownership violate the second amendment of our Constitution, which guarantees individuals the right to possess guns in their homes for self-defense. Our president and some members of Congress believe restrictions are necessary because of the violations carried out in recent years on innocent people by criminally minded, irresponsible, and mentally incompetent citizens using high-powered guns and munitions. The mass murder of school children in Connecticut in 2012 is a prime example.

Many gun owners disagree. They don't think restricting guns would solve the problem. Who will win? The President who wants to prevent murder and thinks his laws will achieve that purpose, or the people who don't believe his restrictions will be effective and do believe he's taking away their rights? As the issue is debated, violence continues and there's a cry for justice.

## Stage Two: We Demand Justice

On the lawns of many citizens of the town where I live is the sign "JUSTICE FOR GARRETT". After returning from school on Oct. 24, 2011, twelve-year-old Garrett Phillips, a fun-loving and friendly middle school student was murdered in his own home. Everyone in my community was shocked. Numerous complaints and demands for justice have been voiced. After two and a-half years, a man in the community was indicted. Then he was released. Now, three years later, he has been re-indicted.[2]

I don't know if he is guilty. Some people are convinced he is; others believe he's not. I believe God will ultimately bring the guilty person to judgment. This is what Scripture says: "Everyone must die once and then be judged" (Hebrews 9:27 NCV). Some people in my town may have given up on that and blame God.

## Stage Three: We Blame and Distrust God/Others

Blaming and distrusting God often happens, especially when justice is slow in coming. People become impatient and take things into their own hands. Though we carry on our money the inscription "IN GOD WE TRUST," our nation has a history of vigilante hangings. I wonder where our trust actually resides. How does trusting God for justice and protection fit in with needing an arsenal of weapons to ensure personal safety? What is wise on our part and what is unnecessary?

Why do we not trust God? Perhaps we believe he is unfair. Perhaps we're envious of what he's given to others and think he's not interested in us. Perhaps we believe he's let us down by allowing us to be hurt. I've believed all of those lies about God at different times in my life.

For years, I thought God was less interested in me than he was my twin sister. During her infancy, she experienced a miraculous healing. During my childhood years, I experienced abuse. I blamed God for allowing that to happen. In my heart I accused him of being unfair. Thinking God is unfair, or unavailable to help us, often propels us into the next stage of revenge.

## Step Four: We Take Justice into Our Hands

When we take justice into our hands we think we know the motives and limitations of our "enemy." And we think that we are capable of dishing out a fair payback. Only God knows the motives of anyone's heart. Unless he shows them to us, we don't even know our own motives.

This is the way (through his prophet Jeremiah) that God described our hearts: "Hopelessly dark and deceitful, a puzzle that no one can figure out. But [he says] I, God, search the heart and examine the mind. I get to the heart of the human. I get to the root of things. I treat them as they really are, not as they pretend to be" (Jeremiah 17: 9–10 MSG).

If my husband yelled at me and put me down (he doesn't), I would feel hurt and offended. It would be right for me to confront him about his behavior, but I could not rightly say to him, "You yelled at me *because* you hate me." That would be an arrogant assumption on my part; I don't know why someone else does what he or she does; I can only guess.

When we take justice into our own hands, we believe that our payback will even out the score, and restore peace in the relationship. But we don't have the ability to discern true guilt, and we don't know how to execute perfect justice. God, in his wisdom and love is the only one who can exact perfect justice. The prophet Isaiah, in describing Jesus, said, "He will not judge by appearance nor make a decision based on hearsay. He will give justice to the poor and make fair decisions for the exploited" (Isaiah 11:3–4 NLT). Nevertheless, whether it's a small offense or a major one, we all can be tempted to take justice into our hands and pay back our offender.

## Stage Five: We Develop a Plan to Get Even

The plan we develop to get even with someone who's hurt us can be conscious or unconscious. If we were wounded during childhood, we probably did not consciously think about how we were coping with the hurt. We just reacted. Yet, we could be stuck in a childish pattern of resentment and subconsciously be acting out our plan of revenge for years. That's the way I lived—until God intervened and opened my eyes.

While working on this chapter I received a phone call from my sister. After a few words, I could think of nothing more to say. It was as if my brain was empty. I felt stuck, and a little bit puzzled. Why did I have nothing to say to my sister? While I was journaling about it the next morning, the Lord showed me that I withdrew from my sister because of hidden resentment in my heart, and it was a way of getting revenge. Revenge for something that had occurred years before! I've done this before, and I often do it. It happens quickly and automatically because it's an old behavior which doesn't require much conscious thought—like driving a car.

When I learned to drive a car, I had to pay close attention to what I was doing. Where was I placing my foot? On the gas pedal or on the brake? How far did I need to turn the steering wheel so that I could get around the corner without running into the curb or into traffic? Which way should I turn the steering wheel when I was backing up? How much force did I need to place on the brake when I wanted to stop the car? After driving the car for many years, I don't have to think about these things. I can relax, carry on a conversation, or write poetry in my head. I *do* notice sharp corners, red lights, stop signs and people walking on the side of the road, but I don't have to think about *how* to get around the corner, *how* to stop the car, or *how* to avoid hitting a pedestrian. I automatically do the right thing.

As an adult, I handled hurt, injustice, and emotional pain in the same way I handled these things as a child. I did not think about what I was doing. I automatically acted and reacted. For years, I traveled down the highway of life, believing I was doing the right thing and thinking I was perfectly safe. I believed I was a forgiving person.

God knew differently. As I talked to him about the puzzling phone call with my sister, he showed me I was a revengeful person and I was traveling down the road of personal destruction. When I was a child and felt abandoned, I withdrew. I took my thoughts and feelings and hid them somewhere inside my head. By refusing to talk (withholding my thoughts and feelings from others), I felt got even.

Withdrawing from others is a form of passive aggression. Passive aggression is one way resentful people get even. It's a common way of handling anger when we feel violated. This kind of behavior enables us to look good; but, at the same time, we remember the offenses done to us—forever. The anger we *think* we are hiding comes out in indirect ways.

## Stage Six: We Fake Friendship

When I don't write or call someone for years, no one can accuse me of revenge. They might think I'm sick or have other extenuating circumstances, that there is a valid reason for my lack of contact. I can delude *myself* into thinking there's a valid reason for my behavior— illness, family or job demands. Whatever excuse I make up for myself, my reactive behavior does not bring about justice.

The point is: such behavior inflicts pain: its consequences are phony and shallow relationships. We can appear to love someone, even give hugs and kisses. But the writer of Proverbs lets us know that kisses don't always indicate love. He said, "The kisses of an enemy are deceitful" (Proverbs 27:6 NKJV).

Judas Iscariot's betrayal kiss of Jesus described in the Gospel of Mark illustrates this proverb.

> Just as he was speaking, Judas, one of the Twelve, appeared. With him was a crowd armed with swords and clubs, sent from the chief priests, the teachers of the law, and the elders. Now the betrayer had arranged a signal with them: "The one I kiss is the man; arrest him and lead him away under guard." Going at once to Jesus, Judas said, "Rabbi!" and kissed him. The men seized Jesus and arrested him.
> —Mark 14: 43–46 (NIV)

Judas's betrayal was not an impulse decision. He planned it and waited for an opportune time to act. This is what revengeful people do. They appear to be cooperative and pleasant but have not forgotten or forgiven the offense and will eventually carry out their hidden agenda.

The Old Testament contains many stories about revengeful people who had hidden agendas. One of them (found in the book of Genesis) is the story of a rape. While visiting friends in a nearby country, a dignitary in that country raped Dinah, one of Jacob's daughters. When her brothers heard about it they were furious and planned to get even. But they hid their anger from the rapist and suggested to him there was a way that he could marry their sister. He went along with their plan and put himself in a vulnerable position. Then Dinah's brothers moved in. They murdered him and his entire family. (Genesis 34:1–31)

## Stage Seven: We Wait For an Opportune Time

Dinah's brothers waited for an opportune time to carry out their revengeful plan. An opportune time to act is the time when the most damage can be exacted. Individuals, families, social groups, political groups, and nations all get caught up in the cycle of revenge. The Islamic extremists who planned the 9/11 attack on New York and Washington D.C. timed it to occur when the largest number of people would be murdered.

Knowing that we have an enemy, but not knowing *when* that enemy is going to attack makes us feel anxious. Satan, the enemy of our souls, does not tell us when he's going to attack us. He's very subtle and waits until we are in a vulnerable position. He chose to tempt Jesus at the end of forty days of fasting when he knew Jesus would be hungry and weak. (Matthew 4) He's still out to get Christians.

In a letter to early Christians, Peter reminds of us this but tells us not to be discouraged and reactive because temptation and suffering are temporary.

> Keep a cool head. Stay alert. The Devil is poised to pounce, and would like nothing better than to catch you napping. Keep your guard up. You're not the only ones plunged into these hard times. It's the same with Christians all over the world. So keep a firm grip on the faith. The suffering won't last forever. It won't be long before this generous God who has great plans for us in Christ—eternal and glorious plans they are!—will have you put together and on your feet for good. He gets the last word; yes, he does.
> —1 Peter 5:8–11 (MSG)

Judas listened to the devil and betrayed Jesus. Eve listened to the devil and ate of the forbidden fruit. The Pharisees (religious leaders of

Jesus' day) listened to the devil, became enraged at Jesus and got him crucified. If we listen to the lies of the devil when we are injured, then we are likely to take things into our own hands and find ways to get even with those who've hurt us. We don't need much help from the devil, though. The sin-nature we've inherited is quite adept at seeking revenge. We must accept responsibility for our choices.

## Stage Eight: We Carry Out Our Plan/Get Even

Getting even supposedly will bring things back into balance but it never does, it only makes things worse. While I was writing on this topic, I listened to a news report detailing events in Afghanistan. Two U.S. marines had burned some copies of the Koran. The furious Afghans felt extremely violated. They proclaimed that President Obama's apology was not enough; there needed to be consequences. What an example of revenge!

## Step Nine: We Experience Higher Levels of Violation, Pain, and Alienation

People caught in revenge are like fighters in a boxing match. They design each punch to inflict damage. How can punches designed to inflict damage result in healing? Violence does not decrease, it escalates. One infamous example of escalating levels of violation is the Hatfield-McCoy feud, which occurred in the 1880's between neighbors in West Virginia. The payback for such things as a stolen pig and a debt owed on a fiddle was arson and murder.[3]

Revenge is a vicious cycle. Stress, anger and destruction increase with each re-payment. As conflicts escalate into higher and higher levels of violation it becomes harder and harder to achieve peace. Increased pain and alienation make us unable to be objective and the cycle of retaliation has no outlet. Days lengthen into months, months into years, years into decades and decades into centuries. Revengeful people are merciless making reconciliation impossible.

The ultimate act of hatred and revenge is the combination of murder/suicide. Vengeful people, by killing others as well as themselves, prevent those they injure from ever getting even, executing justice, or offering forgiveness. Revenge drives the radical terrorist networks that exist throughout the world, as well as many of the lone-wolf killers. Is it possible for individuals and society eradicate it? In the following chapter, I suggest an alternative.

# 14

## Prefer Mercy and Obtain Freedom

> But to you who are willing to listen, I say, love your enemies! Do good to those who hate you. Bless those who curse you. Pray for those who hurt you.
> — Luke 6:27–28 (NLT)

If we are caught up in the cycle of revenge, the declaration made by Jesus Christ that we should do good to, bless, and pray for those who have hurt us probably sounds like a ridiculous impossibility. But Jesus did not make this declaration from a lofty position of safety and inexperience. The things he taught his followers to do, he practiced.

The ultimate act of love and mercy was the death of Jesus Christ. He paid the sin-debt all of us owe, satisfying a just God and making forgiveness and reconciliation possible for everyone. When we accept Christ's gift of mercy and forgiveness, he gives us the promised Holy Spirit. It's our relationship with the Spirit that empowers us to turn from our vengeful behaviors, forgive others, and pursue reconciliation.

The [Development of Mercy](#) drawing [(image 10, p 188, in the Appendix)](#) shows choices that result in forgiveness and make possible reconciliation. In order to receive the grace we need to make these difficult choices we must stay connected to Jesus.

## Stage One: We Suffer Violations/Losses

If we believe everyone will *like* us when we become Christians, we are in for a big surprise. This is Jesus' message to us: "If you find the godless world is hating you, remember it got its start hating me. If you lived on the world's terms, the world would love you as one of its own. But since I picked you to live on God's terms and no longer on the world's terms, the world is going to hate you" (John 15:18–19 MSG).

Accepting this statement is difficult if we come to Christ because we want to *escape* suffering. To make matters worse, it's not only in the world that we experience rejection and pain—we Christians hurt each other; some suffering is a consequence of our *own* actions. Gossip which damages a reputation, extramarital affairs, and abuse are all too common. Nevertheless, God's intention for the Church to be a supportive and loving community has not changed. He is patient with us. The Holy Spirit is with us day and night. He's compassionate and just. When we feel violated we can talk to him about it.

## Stage Two: We Desire Justice

Desiring justice when we have been injured is a healthy response; it's not wrong. We are not called to accept suffering no matter where it's coming from. I've counseled some dear Christians who seem to think so. They misunderstand Christian teachings about submission and think God is pleased with them by their acceptance of control and abuse.

Does God condone abuse? Indeed not! It's a distorted and inaccurate reading of Scriptures that causes us to think so. For example, Christians often quote the first part of the following verse (an injunction against divorce), but ignore the second part of the verse which indicates God hates abuse (violence) as much as divorce. "For I hate divorce, says the Lord, the God of Israel, and covering one's garment with violence, says the LORD of hosts. So take heed to yourselves and do not be faithless" (Malachi 2:16 New Revised Standard Version).

Unfortunately, many Christian pastors, believing marriages should be preserved at all cost, ignore and minimize the effects of abuse. Kay Marshall Strom's book, *In The Name of Submission*, addresses this sad and unscriptural position. She writes,

> Christ never calls us to follow someone into sin, or to support them in their sin. We live in a country where the law clearly states that men are not allowed to batter their wives. Beating up on another person—and that includes a wife—is a felony. A man who physically abuses his wife is a criminal. Because he is breaking civil law, he is also breaking God's law.[1]

Human slavery still exists in many parts of the world, but God never condones it. Again, through the prophet Malachi, this is what he says: "Yes, I'm on my way to visit you with Judgment. I'll present compelling evidence against sorcerers, adulterers, liars, those who exploit workers, those who take advantage of widows and orphans, those who are inhospitable to the homeless—anyone and everyone who doesn't honor me" (Malachi 3:5 MSG).

Though slavery and oppression is still rampant in the earth, God's love for abused people has not ceased. They need never to give up. Their recourse is to trust God for deliverance, and it's the place of those of us in the free world to work for their freedom and safety. Sadly, victims of abuse often live in denial and feel guilty about desiring justice. There's a difference, though, between desiring justice, demanding justice and executing justice—carrying it out.

Is it our job, when we are injured, to demand and execute justice? Though that might be our biggest desire, God's perspective is a little different. This is what he said through his prophet Micah: "He has shown you, O man, what *is* good; and what does the LORD require of you but to *do* justly, to *love* mercy, and to walk humbly with your God" (Micah 6:8 NKJV).

Focusing on the wrong that what we have done (without denying our injury), instead of the wrong that our offender has done, places us in a position to receive God's intervention; we can come to him with confidence and boldness knowing we have grounds for a hearing. He will listen to our prayers. (1 Peter 3:12 NIV) Jesus displayed confidence in God the Father's righteous, fair, and sovereign judgment when he was going through unjust suffering. He did not retaliate to insults or threaten revenge. (1Peter 2:23 NLT)

## Stage Three: We Trust God to be Impartial in Judgment

Despite Jesus' example, most of us do not possess the kind of confidence in God he displayed. Trust is not always our first response. Why? To begin with, we inherited the skepticism of Adam and Eve. In addition, many of us grow up in homes where we have to fend for ourselves.

Sandra Wilson, in her book *Hurt People Hurt People*, explains why children, unprotected in childhood years, struggle with trusting God. She writes,

> If we were born into unstable households, we probably concluded very early that we had to figure out how to keep ourselves safe, since none of the bigger people—mothers and fathers—could be trusted to take care of us in a way that felt genuinely safe . . . We assumed that the heavenly Parent could not be trusted to keep us safe either.[2]

Trusting God, like any other type of growth, is a process. It takes a lot of trust to open up our hearts and share our secrets, fears and failures. Blindness to our own offenses, however, blocks our progress in the Christian life.

## Stage Four: We Acknowledge Our Own Offenses

"That's the pot calling the kettle black," my father would say to me, when I started pointing out a fault in someone else. This idiom, for those of you who find it confusing, referred to a time when cooking was done on a wood-burning stove or over a fire. The bottoms of all the cooking containers were blackened by smoke. My father meant I had no business judging someone else because I was doing the same thing that they were doing.

Jesus said, "The standard you use in judging is the standard by which you will be judged. And why worry about a speck in your friend's eye when you have a log in your own? How can you think of saying to your friend, 'Let me help you get rid of that speck in your eye,' when you can't see past the log in your own eye?" (Matthew 7:2–4 NLT).

Because we all have logs in our eyes, complete impartiality is impossible for us to attain. As I was writing today, God gave me a new insight regarding a verse that I quoted in Chapter 2 of this book ("For *the Lord does* not *see* as man sees; for man looks at the outward appearance, but the LORD looks at the heart.") I previously assumed that the phrase "outward appearance" referred to physical appearance. Now I realize that it could refer to someone's behavior as well as their physical appearance because outward behavior flows from inner motives.

As I've said several times in this book: Only God knows the inner motives of our hearts. We often are unaware of our own motives. That is why David prayed, "Search me, O God, and know my heart;

test me and know my anxious thoughts. Point out anything in me that offends you, and lead me along the path of everlasting life" (Psalm 139: 23–24 NLT).

What happens when we stop focusing on the people who've offended us and ask God to show us our own hearts? We often find that the thing we can't stand in others is the thing we can't stand in ourselves. When we recognize our own need of mercy and forgiveness we become more merciful toward and less judgmental of others.

## Stage Five: We Receive Mercy/ Forgiveness

"I prayed to God in heaven and oft confessed my sin; yet, I never felt forgiven—even though he said I'd been." Those are the lines of a poem I wrote many years ago. They reflect the confusion I had about both forgiveness and guilt.

Guilt, whether it is false guilt or true guilt (I'll discuss these concepts in my second book of this series), is an uncomfortable feeling. Feeling guilty, though, does not necessarily mean that we *are* guilty, and *not* feeling guilty does not necessarily mean we are innocent. For those of us who tend to make conclusions based on our feelings, this might be difficult to grasp. If we have a condemning conscience, then we will continue to feel guilt, anxiety and fear, even though we've been forgiven. Forgiveness, rightly understood, *does* release us from guilt. It brings us joy, but our joy is not always immediate. Our joy develops and increases through a process which involves both knowledge and faith, as shown through the following illustration.

During my childhood years, when I said, "I'm sorry," I was told, "It's okay, but just don't do it again." Consequently, I developed a belief that forgiveness was based on my effort and ability to be perfect rather than God's unconditional love and grace. I did not feel forgiven unless I could assure myself I would *never* do it again.

To experience the joy of being forgiven we must recognize that achieving perfection is impossible, acknowledge our failures, stop placing faith in our good works, examine the accuracy of our conscience, and place our confidence in the words of Scripture.

Being forgiven fills our hearts with gratitude and love, as well as joy. The Gospel of Luke (7:44–47 NKJV) illustrates this truth. Jesus, in responding to a Pharisee, named Simon who was looking down his nose at a woman he regarded as sinful, said these words:

> Do you see this woman? I entered your house; you gave Me no water for My feet, but she has washed My feet with her tears and wiped them with the hair of her head. You gave Me no kiss, but this woman has not ceased to kiss My feet since the time I came in. You did not anoint My head with oil, but this woman has anointed My feet with fragrant oil. Therefore I say to you, her sins, which are many, are forgiven, for she loved much. But to whom little is forgiven, the same loves little.

Jesus' point was not that the woman was a greater sinner than Simon, but that she recognized her sinfulness and Simon did not. The extent to which we recognize and confess our sin and dysfunction is the extent to which we experience joy through receiving forgiveness. Receiving forgiveness humbles us and wipes out our need to get even.

## Stage Six: We Relinquish Our Right to Get Even

Giving up the right to get even is the practical admission that we are trusting God to bring about justice. Why is it hard to give up that right? To begin with, we believe it's a legitimate right. It's not. As discussed earlier, God is the only one capable of making things fair. The Scriptures declare that vengeance belongs to him, not to us. (Romans 12:9)

Another reason we may not be willing to let go of our right to get even is that we think our injury is too insignificant for God to bother with. Will not God, who notes a sparrow's fall and knows the number of hairs on our head (Matthew 10:28–31) take care of what seems to us an insignificant matter? Sometimes we lack the patience we need to wait until God's time. We want justice *now*, not tomorrow. We insist on seeing justice before we move on, but this mindset *keeps* us from moving on. It puts us on hold. And we could be on hold for the rest of life, because God does not adjust his timetable to fit our schedule.

God is merciful, as well as just; therefore, he gives people an opportunity to change before bringing judgment upon them. (2 Peter 3:9) Believing that God will bring about justice in his time and in his way gives us an opportunity to grow in faith and move into forgiveness.

## Stage Seven: We Forgive Our Offender(s)

Forgiveness, though not easy and often misunderstood, is vital to our mental, emotional, physical and spiritual health. Through holding unforgiveness in our hearts, we torture ourselves *mentally* and *emotionally*—our memories constantly remind us of the injuries others have done to us, and we feel the pain all over again each time we relive the memory. Through refusing to forgive, we injure ourselves *physically*— an increased level of adrenalin (the stress hormone) over time can be a factor in producing chronic illnesses such as high blood pressure, diabetes, arthritis, and ulcers. And, in a life-long refusal to forgive others, we commit spiritual suicide—separate ourselves forever from God's presence and love.

Jesus conditioned receiving forgiveness from our Heavenly Father upon our willingness to forgive others. When we pray (using the words of the Lord's Prayer), "Forgive us our debts, as we also have forgiven our debtors" (Matthew 6:12 NIV), we are not saying, "God, forgive my debts, *then* I will forgive others." We are saying, "Look at my heart, God, I've forgiven my debtors; now, will you forgive me?"

God does look at our hearts, and he knows whether or not we are speaking truthfully. To declare I've forgiven someone means I've forgiven him (or her) from my heart. What does it mean to forgive from my heart? It doesn't mean I have a warm *feeling* toward someone. It means I've changed my heart belief. When I change my heart belief, my feelings will eventually change.

Jesus illustrated what it means to change a heart belief in one of his parables. He told a story about a man who owed a debt that was impossible for him to pay. His angry creditor threatened to throw him and his family into jail. The man pleaded for mercy and his creditor forgave the entire debt. However, the forgiven man went out and grabbed a person who owed him very little and threw him in jail. Then the original creditor had the first man thrown into jail to be tortured until he could repay his debt. Jesus said, "This is how my heavenly Father will treat each of you unless you forgive your brother or sister from your heart" (Matthew 18:35 NIV).

Therefore, if we want to be forgiven by God, we must take forgiving others seriously. Still, forgiveness is seldom easy or quick, and most of us don't really understand what it means. It's much more than speaking the words, "I forgive you."

I memorized The Lord's Prayer as a child. Learning to practice forgiveness has taken many years. Maybe part of the reason I did not feel forgiven was that in my heart I carried a load of unforgiveness. Forgiveness is often more likely to be a process than a one-time event.

Stoop and Masteller, in their book, *Forgiving Our Parents, Forgiving Ourselves*, describe the process of forgiveness in detail, listing and discussing the following six steps:

- Recognize the injury.
- Identify the emotions involved.
- Express your hurt and anger.
- Set boundaries to protect yourself.
- Cancel the debt.
- Consider the possibility of reconciliation.[3]

Canceling a debt, possibly the most difficult stage of forgiveness, is made easier when we recognize the size of our own debt before God and how impossible it is for any of us to pay him back. Paying our debt cost God the death of his son.

All of the steps of forgiveness are essential and we can get stuck on any of them. I've struggled with one or another at different stages of my life and with different people in my life. Working through them, difficult as it may be, continues to bring me freedom and joy. Forgiveness is the opposite of paying back. Instead of reacting to an insult by slinging back with another insult, God tells us to speak a blessing.

## Stage Eight: We Bless Our Offender(s)

Blessing an offender goes beyond forgiveness; it's the litmus test that indicates whether or not our forgiveness is genuine. However, if we want to have an intimate relationship with our heavenly Father, if we want to be mature, we must replace hatred with love and vengeance with blessing. This is what Jesus instructed his disciples to do: "Love your enemies and pray for those who persecute you, that you may be children of your Father in heaven. He causes his sun to rise on the evil and the good, and sends rain on the righteous and the unrighteous.

If you love those who love you, what reward will you get" (Matthew 5:44–46 NIV)?

Another reason for blessing our offenders is that in *not* doing so we may be unaware of the unforgiveness and vengeance still in our hearts which will keep God from answering our prayers. Blessing others insures us of God's blessing. These are the instructions given to us by Peter: "Finally, all of you, have unity of mind, sympathy, brotherly love, a tender heart, and a humble mind. Do not repay evil for evil or reviling for reviling, but on the contrary, bless, for to this you were called, that you may obtain a blessing" (1 Peter 3:8–10 NKJV).

Even after we have forgiven someone, it may be difficult to bless that person unless we have assurance that we will not be hurt again. Can we bless someone who has hurt us and remain safe? These questions relate to having boundaries.

## Stage Nine: We Set Boundaries and Work toward Reconciliation

A friend of mine has a daughter who is very critical of her. My friend has set a boundary that she will not listen to the abuse for hours and hours upon end. She has not cut off the relationship. She knows she can't control her daughter's tongue, yet she doesn't have to listen to critical remarks which wound her soul. She prays for her daughter and reaches out to her in many ways, but she does not set herself up for continued abuse. She continues to forgive her daughter, but they are not reconciled.

Reconciliation is not the same as forgiveness. Reconciliation goes beyond forgiveness but it's not always possible. Reconciliation involves trust. And we can't force someone to trust us.

In Paul Hegstrom's life story (*Angry Men and the Women Who Love Them*), he gives an example of how effective boundaries enabled him to reconcile with his wife after four years of separation. He began by establishing a friendship, and lists four levels in the development of a friendship—acquaintance, casual, close, intimate.

At first his wife would only meet with him at a restaurant where she felt safe. She would not allow him to pick her up and she always sat in a place where she could easily get to the door if she felt threatened. Later she agreed to join him with a group of friends. When she felt safe enough, she began riding in the car with him.

These are the skills he discusses for building and restoring a relationship:

- Become friends.
- Become safe in the ability to express yourself, your needs, and your pain.
- Know you are safe to do this.
- Don't be in a reactive mood.
- Identify issues and work through them.[4]

Even when our offenders do not seek it, we can choose to forgive them. In order to reconcile with them, they must also desire it and be willing to work toward it. Is it possible to reconcile without truly forgiving? Yes, it is but, according to Christian psychologists Stoop and Masteller, this leads only to artificial reconciliation and increased pain in the relationship.

Artificial reconciliation happens when we act in the following ways:

- overlook the pain caused by someone's actions
- deny we've been hurt
- excuse inexcusable behavior
- fear we'll lose the relationship if we speak up.[4]

In the following paragraphs, Steph shares how the concepts in this chapter helped her make a difficult decision based on mercy rather than revenge.

> While I was in Jane's Bible/book study class, covering this book, I was faced with the decision of whether I should travel to my sister's wedding across the country. Using Jane's "Map of Revenge" and "Development of Mercy" illustrations, I was able to make my decision and be at peace with it.
>
> At that time, I felt violated by my sister for a multitude of reasons. Through Jane's teachings, I was able to recognize my dysfunctional behavior that I have defaulted to in the past. I have shut down and felt that communicating my feelings is pointless because the person gives me excuses for why it is okay for what they did. I also shut down, because I hate arguing, so instead I give up. When I shut down, I distance myself from the problem because I feel that the person doesn't care that they hurt me; they say I am being too demanding or sensitive or unreasonable. I also sometimes pretend that things are okay, and then I find that I resent the person for believing me. I now realize that this behavior is dysfunctional since I am not being honest with myself or the other person.
>
> Rather than seek justice, or put myself in a situation that would leave me feeling further violated, I sought to create peace. Although I could not force my sister to live in a peaceable situation, I chose to make my decision based on how to create peace for my family and myself. I relinquished my right to get even, forgave how my sister had offended me and blessed her and her new husband.

By first doing these steps, I can honestly say that my decision to not travel across the country and outlay precious financial, emotional and physical resources, was one that I am at peace with. I weighed if I was to attend, would my efforts be appreciated, or would I be placing myself in a martyr-like position, leaving myself in an emotionally defenseless place, needing her approval in order to feel accepted. I did not want to blame God if I chose to make the decision to go, and find that I had been violated once again. God does not want us to be victims of destructive relationships. Instead, I chose to use self-control to set healthy boundaries that were based on reasonable expectations, which led me to avoid a stressful climatic situation.

By using Jane's Maps of Revenge and Mercy, I was able to set reasonable expectations for myself, which is something I struggle with. I try to do more than I should, and then feel resentful when my efforts go unnoticed. I was able to realize that I am responsible for the choices that I make that lead me to feel unrecognized. If I knowingly place myself in an emotionally stressful and violating situation, then I am self-victimizing myself. An action like that is not Christ-like. God wants us to use wisdom and prayer to be equipped to serve Him in His kingdom.

Forgiveness can be one-sided. We can forgive our offenders even if they do not forgive us, but reconciliation must be mutual. The sad news is: it might not be possible for us to reconcile with all of our offenders. Sometimes it's dangerous and unwise for us to do so. Other times, those we have offended might not be willing to forgive and accept us.

The good news is: though we've offended God more than anyone could offend us, Christ paid our debt; "God was reconciling the world to himself in Christ, not counting people's sins against them . . . "God made him who had no sin to be sin for us, so that in him we might become the righteousness of God" (2 Corinthians 5:19, 21 NIV).

He offers forgiveness and reconciliation, but it's not automatic. We must accept his offer. This is what we must do to become reconciled with God:

- Truthfully confess our offenses.
- Repent of them (have heart change, as well as a change of direction).
- Receive his merciful forgiveness, love and grace.

We can accept his mercy or not, but the debt we owe God can never be paid for by any of our good works. Knowing we are forgiven, cleansed from guilt and accepted by him brings us unimaginable joy and freedom. The weird thing is that some of us, having been forgiven by God and reconciled with him still struggle with anxiety and guilt. I discuss why that might happen in Book Two of this series.

# STUDY GUIDE

This guide is designed to help you understand the concepts found in the book *Emotional Freedom: The Choices You Must Make* and apply them to everyday life situations. For each chapter in the book, you will find a corresponding section containing the following two items: a <u>Key Concepts</u> list that summarizes the contents of the chapter and <u>Questions for Reflection and Discussion.</u> Included in the <u>Questions for Reflection and Discussion</u> section of some chapters you will find <u>Opportunities for Journaling</u>.

Journaling is simply placing your prayer on paper. It's not about writing a formal prayer. It's about telling God what you are thinking and feeling, asking questions, and inviting him to give you wisdom and understanding. The purpose of telling Jesus about your thoughts and feelings is not to inform him about them, but to face them, yourself. If you've never done any journaling, don't like to write, believe you can't write, or feel intimidated by writing, I hope you will not let these problems keep you from beginning this discipline. Don't be concerned about using correct grammar and spelling. I don't believe that God cares a lot about that.

Although you could work through this guide on your own, doing so with a small group of friends might be very beneficial. You could discover that you are not alone in your struggles and receive the encouragement and prayer support that trusted friends can provide.

# 1. Oaks of Righteousness

## Key Concepts:

- God's destiny for broken-hearted, weak, emotionally dishonest, resentful, unforgiving, and fearful people filled with shame is to become "Oaks of Righteousness."
- "Oak of Righteousness" is the identity of all followers of Jesus Christ who are undergoing Holy Spirit empowered character transformation—developing the emotional and moral integrity of Jesus Christ
- Emotional integrity means we don't pretend to be something we are not, and we don't hide behind a wall of self-protection.
- Moral integrity means we choose the pathway of love—making decisions based on love rather than convenience—and stick to them even when it costs us something.
- Emotional and moral integrity are necessary for the development of Christ-like character.

## Questions for Reflection and Discussion

1. What struggles do you have in regard to maintaining moral and/or emotional integrity?

2. Do you have a self-protective wall?
   A. If so, what are its advantages?

   B. What are its disadvantages?

Jesus' disciple, John, tells us that if we want to become spiritually mature, we must have emotional integrity—be truthful about our moral failures (sins). Read his words and answer questions 3 and 4.

> If we claim that we're free of sin, we're only fooling ourselves. A claim like that is errant nonsense. On the other hand, if we admit our sins—make a clean breast of them—he won't let us down; he'll be true to himself. He'll forgive our sins and purge us of all wrongdoing. If we claim that we've never sinned, we out-and-out contradict God—make a liar out of him. A claim like that only shows off our ignorance of God.
> —1 John 1:8–10 (MSG)

3. What does God promise to us when we come out from behind our self-protective walls?

4. What are the dangers of concealing our destructive emotions, such as anger, resentment and revenge?

Although we need to be transparent and truthful in order to grow, it's not wise in every situation. We need to be and feel safe. Read the following advice, think about it, and then answer questions 5 and 6.
"Wounds from a friend can be trusted, but an enemy multiplies kisses" (Proverbs 27:6 NIV).
"A prudent person sees trouble coming and ducks; a simpleton walks in blindly and is clobbered" (Proverbs 27:12 MSG).

5. Write down the name of someone whom you know you can trust, and think about what you might want to share with that person.

6. If you are doing this study with a group of friends, what do you need from that group in order to feel safe?

Read Isaiah 61:1–3 (the Scripture about our destiny that's quoted in chapter one), ask the Lord to speak to your heart, and then answer questions 7–9.

7. What words of Scripture stood out to you?

8. What desires and feelings did you have as you mediated on Isaiah 61?

9. What would you like to say to God in response to what you read?

10. Journal Opportunity: Write a prayer, telling God what you think and how you feel about the concepts of Chapter 1.

## 2. Aborted and Diseased "Fruit"

### Key Concepts:

- Because we lack the power to follow through with our good intentions, we 'abort' our good desires and give in to destructive desires and emotions.
- We don't understand what makes us so powerlessness.
- Jesus lived with the same limitations that we have, yet he did not yield to destructive desires—even once.

- A primary reason for our failure to follow through with good intentions is that we don't understand the complexity of our emotions.

## Questions for Reflection and Discussion

Read the following Scripture and answer questions 1–6.

> "I decide to do good, but I don't really do it; I decide not to do bad, but then I do it anyway. My decisions, such as they are, don't result in actions. Something has gone wrong deep within me and gets the better of me every time"
>
> (Romans 7:19–20 MSG).

1. Which are you more aware of in yourself: "Not doing the good" or "doing the bad?" Give some examples.

2. Which seems worse to you? Explain your answer.

3. Give a recent example of a "good" that you failed to follow through on?

4. How do you *feel* when you don't follow through on a good intention?

5. What do you say to yourself when you fail to follow through on your good intentions?

6. Sometimes, when we don't follow through on our good intentions, we say to ourselves: "God doesn't expect perfection." Do you think this statement is helpful or unhelpful? Explain your answer.

When Jesus said "You are to be perfect, even as your Father in heaven is perfect" (Matthew 5:48 NLT), he used the Greek word *telios* which means mature. This word refers to inward character change, not simply outward behavior.

7. Why do you think Jesus emphasized inward character change rather than outward behavior changes?

Jesus *always* responded to the frustrations and difficulties of life with love, joy, peace, patience, kindness, goodness, faithfulness, gentleness, and self-control. Although, we are growing, we are inconsistent in displaying these characteristics. To discover what we (in time) will be like, read the following Scripture; and then answer questions 8–10. "Dear friends, now we are children of God, and what we will be has not yet been made known. But we know that when Christ appears we shall be like him, for we shall see him as he is. All who have this hope in him purify themselves, just as he is pure" (I John 3:2–3 NIV).

8. How do these words of Scripture make you feel?

9. In what ways do you want to become more like Jesus?

10. What, specifically, does this verse motivate you to do?

## 3. The "Tree" Model of Emotion

### Key Concepts:

The development of emotions and desires is complex. It's helpful to think of them as trees.

- Roots represent our core (heart) beliefs.
- The trunk and branches represent our conscious thought life.
- Leaves represent our feelings.
- Fruit represents our behavior: words, actions, and attitudes.
- Our genetic predisposition influences the way we express emotions; for example, people of Scandinavian descent tend to be less expressive than those of Italian descent.
- The soil in which an emotion tree is planted represents generational influence; the patterns of thinking and behavior that existed in our family of origin affect the development of our emotions.
- The climate that surrounds an emotion tree represents the social environment in which we live: family, job, local community, and world; this, also affects the development and expression of emotions.

### Questions for Reflection and Discussion

To help you understand the concepts found in this chapter, review the "Tree" Model of Emotion drawing (Image 1 in the Appendix).

Look at the "soil" in which you were planted; that is, think about what you learned from your family of origin about managing anger, anxiety, resentment, and revenge; then, answer questions 1 and 2.

1. What was helpful?

2. What was unhelpful?

3. Which of these emotions—anger, resentment or revenge—are easy for you to identify in yourself, and which ones are more difficult to identify?

4. Were there any "forbidden" emotions in your family? If so, what were they?

Read the following passage from the Book of Psalms, which records one of David's prayers and then, answer questions 4, 5, and 6.

> "Turn to me and have mercy, for I am alone and in deep distress. My problems go from bad to worse. Oh, save me from them all! Feel my pain and see my trouble. Forgive all my sins"
> (Psalm 25:16–18 NLT).

4. In comparison with David, to what extend do you share your feelings with God?

5. If you do not share your feelings with God, what do you think keeps you from doing so?

6. How do you think you might benefit by sharing your feelings with God?

Proverbs says, "For as he thinks in his heart, so *is* he" (23:7 NKJV).

7. Write down six things that in your heart you believe about yourself (your "root" beliefs).

In the book of Philippians, Paul gives some guidelines for evaluating whether or not our thoughts are healthy. He states the criteria for healthy thoughts in the following verse.

> "Fix your thoughts on what is true, and honorable, and right, and pure, and lovely, and admirable. Think about things that are excellent and worthy of praise" (Phil. 4:8 NLT).

8. Look at the beliefs about yourself that you listed in question 7 and check off the ones that meet the criteria for healthy thoughts.

Journal Opportunity: Talk to the Lord about any unhealthy beliefs that you have about yourself and ask him to tell you what you could replace them with.

## 4. Disconnection from the "Well"

### Key Concepts:

- Like Adam and Eve, we've listened to Satan's destructive lies about God, ourselves, and others.

- We've allowed these lies to take root in our hearts, rejected God as our source of power and joy, and chose to become our own ultimate authority.
- Consequently, we experience a deep spiritual thirst which nothing can satisfy.

## Questions for Reflection and Discussion

Read the following Scripture from Genesis; and then, answer questions 1–5.

> Now the snake was the most clever of all the wild animals the LORD God had made. One day the snake said to the woman, "Did God really say that you must not eat fruit from any tree in the garden?"
> The woman answered the snake, "We may eat fruit from the trees in the garden. But God told us, 'You must not eat fruit from the tree that is in the middle of the garden. You must not even touch it, or you will die.'"
> But the snake said to the woman, "You will not die. God knows that if you eat the fruit from that tree, you will learn about good and evil and you will be like God!"
> —Genesis 3:1–5 (NCV)

1. When he spoke to Eve, in what ways did the serpent (Satan) make God "look bad" to her?

2. In what ways, either now or in the past, has Satan made God "look bad" to you?

3. Why do you think the promise that she would be like God was so attractive to Eve?

4. What does being your own "god" look like for you?

5. What are the consequences when you turn away from God and go your own way?

Read the following Scripture and then, answer question 6.

> "Trust in the LORD with all your heart; do not depend on your own understanding.
> Seek his will in all you do, and he will show you which path to take.
> Don't be impressed with your own wisdom. Instead, fear the LORD and turn away from evil.
> Then you will have healing for your body and strength for your bones" Proverbs
> (3:5–8 NLT).

6. What are the benefits of trusting in God and living according to his wisdom?

Read the following two Scriptures (The first one describes Satan; the second one describes Jesus) and then, answer questions 7 and 8. "Keep a cool head. Stay alert. The Devil is poised to pounce, and would like nothing better than to catch you napping" (I Peter 5:8 MSG). "The thief's purpose is to steal and kill and destroy. My purpose is to give them a rich and satisfying life. "I am the good shepherd. The good shepherd sacrifices his life for the sheep" (John 10: 10–11 NLT).

7. What do these verses tell you about the character of Satan?

8. What do these verses tell you about the character of Jesus?

Journal Opportunity: Talk to Jesus about any problems you have with trusting him. Ask him to show you any lies about him that you've believed, and invite him to show you the truth about himself.

## 5. Bonded to a Diseased Root

### Key Concepts:

- When we reject our Creator-God's rightful, wise, and compassionate authority, we live in bondage to a cruel dictator called the sin nature.
- We become slaves to its destructive desires and passions—such as anger, bitter resentment, and merciless revenge.
- Like a chained handcuff attached to our wills, it prevents us from doing the good we want to do and compels us to do the bad that we don't want to do.

## Questions for Reflection and Discussion

To help you understand the concepts presented in this chapter, review the Bondage to a Diseased Root diagram (Image 2 in the Appendix).

1. The following list of characteristics describes us when we live under the control of the sin nature. Match each characteristic with the Scripture that describes it. A specific Bible version

is not always suggested; if you read several versions, you will gain more understanding. (You can find a list of translations at Biblegateway.com)

The following list of characteristics describes us when we live under the control of the sin nature. Match each characteristic with the Scripture that describes it.

\_\_\_Deceitful
\_\_\_Desperately wicked
\_\_\_Suppresses (hates) truth
\_\_\_Ungrateful
\_\_\_Hates exposure
\_\_\_Gets progressively worse
\_\_\_Blames others
\_\_\_Pleases others rather than God
\_\_\_Unfaithful, unmerciful
\_\_\_A slave to passions and desires
\_\_\_ Blind
\_\_\_Denies and covers up sin.

A. Hebrews 3:13
B. Proverbs 16:25
C. I John 1:8
D. Titus 3:3
E. John 3:20
F. Genesis 3:12–13
G. Romans 1:18
H. Jeremiah 17:9
I. Ephesians 4:22 (NASB)
J. Romans 1:21
K. Romans 1:31 (NIV)
L. Genesis 3:16–17 (MSG)

2. Which of these characteristics do you give in to, most often?

The following list of characteristics describes the way Jesus lived when he occupied a body just like ours. Match each characteristic with the Scripture that describes it.

___Full of truth
___Loved righteousness, hated wickedness
___Exposed sin
___Was always thankful
___Honored Father-God
___Controlled (led) by the Holy Spirit
___Always obedient to the will of the Father
___Always pleased his Father
___Merciful and compassionate

A. Hebrews 1:9
B. John 8:49
C. John 8:31–41
D. John 1:14
E. John 5:30
F. Matthew 4:1
G. I Corinthians 11:23–24
H. John 6:38
I. Hebrews 4:14–16

3. Which characteristic of Jesus would you most like to have him display in your life?

# 6. Transplanted into Healthy Soil

## Key Concepts:

- God loves us despite our rebellion.
- Living in the contaminated soil of the sin nature, we can't develop into the beautiful and fruitful person God designed us to become.
- Neither positive thinking nor faith in ourselves is strong enough to free us from the power of the sin nature.
- Jesus paid our debt and freed us from the destructive power of the sin nature.
- If we want to live and prosper, we must be transplanted into the healthy soil of God's love.
- Yet, the choice is ours. God doesn't force us to accept his gift of forgiveness and freedom.

## Questions for Reflection and Discussion

1. Review the <u>Transplanted into a Healthy Root</u> diagram (<u>Image 3 in the Appendix</u>) and read the following Scriptures.

Each one describes a choice that we must make in order to be transplanted into the soil of God's love. Write down the choice that each Scripture calls us to make?

    A. Acts 16:31

    B. Romans 10:9–10

    C. Luke 15:3–7

    D. Luke 15:11–24

    E. 2 Corinthians 7:10

Jesus said (Luke 19:10 (NIV), "For the Son of Man came to seek and to save the lost."

2. What does "lost" mean to you?

3. In what way(s) are (were) you lost and need (needed) Jesus to save you?

Read the following description of a relationship with Jesus. Then, answer questions 4 and 5.

> Are you tired? Worn out? Burned out on religion? Come to me. Get away with me and you'll recover your life. I'll show you how to take a real rest. Walk with me and work with me—watch how I do it. Learn the unforced rhythms of grace. I won't lay anything heavy or ill-fitting on you. Keep company with me and you'll learn to live freely and lightly.
> —Matthew 11:28–30 (MSG)

4. What words or phrases in the above paragraph sound most appealing to you?

5. What would it mean for you to "recover your life"?

<u>Journal Opportunity</u>: Talk to Jesus about any needs you are aware of and tell him what your desires are.

# 7. A Dynamic Dance with the Gardener

## Key Concepts:

- We become emotionally healthy through a relationship with the Holy Spirit (Jesus' presence within us).
- The sin nature does not disappear when we connect with Jesus.
- We must actively choose to reject its lies and replace them with truth.
- We develop a "Jesus-kind-of integrity" by this change in our thinking.
- It's God's endless grace that gives us the power to make these changes and develop emotional integrity; we cannot do it through self-reformation is insufficient.
- Yet, we are responsible to choose grace. Grace is God's step of love toward us. Responsibility is our step of love toward God.

## Questions for Reflection and Discussion

1. Read Philippians 2:12–13 and then give an example of how God causes you to do his will.

2. Practically speaking, what does it mean for you to "work out your salvation"?

3. Which of these slogans, "Let go and let God" or "Just say No!" do you tend to live by, and what are the effects in your life?

Read the following Scripture, review the <u>We Must Choose Our Dance Partner</u> diagram (<u>Image 4 in the Appendix</u>), and then answer questions 4–6.

> "Even before he made the world, God loved us and chose us in Christ to be holy and without fault in his eyes"
>
> (Eph. 1:4 NLT).

4. According to Eph. 1:4, being in Christ means "to be holy and without fault." If you thought of yourself as being holy and without fault, how do you think it would affect your behavior?

5. What would you stop doing?

6. What would you start doing?

The following verse tells us what must happen for emotional/spiritual transformation. Read the verse. Then, answer question 7.

> "Don't copy the behavior and customs of this world, but let God transform you into a new person by changing the way you think"
>
> (Romans 12:2 NLT).

7. What is your part in this transformation?

8. What is God's part in this transformation?

In the following Scripture, Jesus described how dependent we are on a relationship with him. Read the verse; then, answer questions 9 and 10.

> "I am the Vine, you are the branches. When you're joined with me and I with you, the relation intimate and organic, the harvest is sure to be abundant. Separated, you can't produce a thing"
>
> (John 15:5 MSG).

9. Does dependence on God seem like a positive or negative thing, and what makes it so?

10. In terms of dependence, how would you describe your current relationship with Jesus?

## 8. Nutrients for Growth

### Key Concept:

We position ourselves to receive God's empowering grace by practicing spiritual disciplines. They following disciplines are basic.

- Prayer-journaling
- Bible study
- Faith-motivated obedience
- Truth-inspired worship
- Restorative rest
- Grace-filled accountability

## Questions for Reflection and Discussion

1. Which of the above disciplines are you currently practicing, and which ones do you have difficulty with?

2. Which discipline you would you like to begin or grow stronger in? What step could you make to get started?

3. If you are doing this study in a group, in what ways would you like members of this group to encourage you in your practice of these disciplines? If you are not in a group, think about where you could find some grace-filled accountability.

Read the following Scripture and then answer question 4.

> Do what God's teaching says; when you only listen and do nothing, you are fooling yourselves. Those who hear God's teaching and do nothing are like people who look at themselves in a mirror. They see their faces and then go away and quickly forget what they looked like. But the truly happy people are those who carefully study God's perfect law that makes people free, and they continue to study it. They do not forget what they heard, but they obey what God's teaching says. Those who do this will be made happy.
> —James 1:22–25 (NCV)

4. What practical things can you do to make sure that you are acting on what God says to you in his Word?

5. In the following Scripture quotation, Jesus is talking to his disciples. Read the quotation and answer the following questions.

> There is so much more I want to tell you, but you can't bear it now. When the Spirit of truth comes, he will guide you into all truth. He will not speak on his own but will tell you what he has heard. He will tell you about the future. He will bring me glory by telling you whatever he receives from me. All that belongs to the Father is mine; this is why I said, 'The Spirit will tell you whatever he receives from me.
> —John 16:12–15 (NLT)

A. Where and how does the Holy Spirit get the "Truth" he gives to us, and to whom does he give credit?

B. What does this tell us about the character of the Holy Spirit?

C. What practical things can you do to help you hear the Holy Spirit's voice?

Read the following Scripture and answer questions 6–9.

> The true children of God are those who let God's Spirit lead them. The Spirit we received does not make us slaves again to fear; it makes us children of God. With that Spirit we cry out, "Father." And the Spirit himself joins with our spirits to say we are God's children. If we are God's children, we will receive blessings from God together with Christ. But we must

suffer as Christ suffered so that we will have glory as Christ has glory.
—Romans 8:14–17 (NCV)

6. What is the Holy Spirit's part in making it safe and comfortable for us to open up our hearts to God?

7. What practical thing(s) could you do so that your worship of God is based on the truth of Scripture rather than the inconsistency of your feelings?

8. What activities strengthen your body, inspire your mind, and renew your spirit?

9. Which of the activities that you listed in question 8 are you practicing on a regular basis, and which of them do you need to begin (or re-begin)?

Journal Opportunity: Talk to God about the disciplines in today's lesson. Tell him what you struggle with and how you want to grow. Listen to him and write down what you believe he says to you.

## 9. Identify Dysfunctional Anger

### Key Concepts:

- Anger is a normal God-given emotion.

- Outward expressions of anger that are destructive (harmful) to others (or yourself) are dysfunctional and out-of-line with God's purposes.
- Denying the presence of (hidden) anger is, also, harmful and destructive.
- Understanding stages in the development of anger, the emotional and physical "soil" that supports it, as well as our "root" beliefs helps us recognize our dysfunctional choices.

## Questions for Reflection and Discussion

Review the "Map of Destructive Anger" diagram (Image 5 in the Appendix), showing the stages of anger; then, answer questions 1-4.

1. Which stage of anger do you tend to become stuck in?

2. How do you express your anger? Do you implode (get angry toward yourself) or explode?

3. Why do you think you make this choice?

4. To help us "cool-down" after we explode, we need to give ourselves distance—some time and space so that our reasoning ability can return. What practical things do you do (or could you do) in order to give yourself that needed distance?

5. Review the Type-A personality characteristics listed in chapter 9 and write down the characteristics that describe you.

6. Choose the one characteristic that you believe is most destructive and write down the first action step you need to take to eliminate it.

How we experience anger and what we are taught about it, early in life, shape our beliefs about anger.

7. What did you learn about anger from the family in which you grew up?

8. How does this affect the way that you handle anger, today?

Read the following Scripture verse on the topic of anger, ask the Holy Spirit to give you understanding, and answer questions 9.

> "Understand this, my dear brothers and sisters: You must all be quick to listen, slow to speak, and slow to get angry"
>
> (James 1:19 NLT).

9. How might listening before you speak reduce the intensity of your anger?

Read the following verse and answer question 10.

> "And don't sin by letting anger control you." Don't let the sun go down while you are still angry, for anger gives a foothold to the devil"
>
> (Ephesians 4:25–27 NLT).

10. In what way does anger give an advantage to the devil?

Journal Opportunity: Think of an occasion when anger controlled you. Use this as an opportunity to pray and journal, asking the Lord to give you understanding of your heart beliefs and any stressors that contributed to that anger.

## 10. Choose Self-control and Become Productive

### Key Concepts:

- Admitting to our destructive expressions of anger is the first step to making positive changes.
- Learning to detect signs of stress in our bodies helps us detect anger.
- Doing something to calm ourselves decreases adrenaline and reduces the intensity of our anger.
- By asking God for wisdom and following the direction of the Holy Spirit, we can use the energy of anger for constructive problem solving.
- We can learn to communicate our anger in ways that improve relationships.
- Resolving anger on a daily basis prevents emotional "baggage" from accumulating in our lives and frees up our energy, so that we become more productive.

### Questions for Reflection and Discussion

Review the Development of Self-Control (Constructive Anger) diagram (Image 6 in the Appendix) then answer questions 1–4.

1. What stage do you need the most help with?

2. What is the first step you could take to find help?

Read the following Scripture, pray for understanding, and answer questions 3 and 4.

> "Be angry, and do not sin. Meditate within your heart on your bed, and be still.
> Offer the sacrifices of righteousness, and put your trust in the LORD."
> (Psalm 4:4–5 NLT).

3. What do you think "meditating within your heart" means?

4. How could silence and mediation help you develop self-control?

Anger often develops as a result of distrust. Distrust is an expression of fear. Distrust can cause us to hide our failures and weaknesses, because we fear we will be rejected and/or abandoned if we admit to them. If we believe God is a strict judge who expects perfection, we might be angry with him and hide our failures. Read the following Scripture, which describes God's attitude toward us when we fail. Then, answer questions 5 and 6.

> "The LORD is compassionate and merciful, slow to get angry and filled with unfailing love.
> He will not constantly accuse us, nor remain angry forever. He does not punish us for all our sins; he does not deal harshly with us, as we deserve"
> (Psalm 103:8–10 NLT).

5. List the words and phrases in the above verse that are used to describe God's behavior and attitudes related to anger.

6. Circle any words and phrases that you listed in question 5 that you would like to "grow" in.

The short Old Testament Book, Jonah, is the story of a man who was very angry at God. Read the four chapters of the Book of Jonah from your favorite Bible translation (or several translations) and answer the questions 7 and 8.

7. Compare the way God handles his anger (See Psalm 103, quoted in question 4) with the way Jonah handled his anger.

8. What expectations do you have for God, for others, and for yourself, that might contribute to your level of anger?

## 11. Uncover Bitter Resentment

### Key Concepts:

- When conflicts reoccur, problems remain unresolved, and losses accumulate, our mounting frustration can develop into resentment.
- Because it "lives underground, we can be unaware of our resentment.
- Becoming aware of how we indirectly lash out can help us identify our hidden resentment.

- Nourishing self-pity and a victim mindset robs us of the ability to problem-solve.
- If we fail to recognize, acknowledge, and address our resentment, bitterness will enslave us.

## Questions for Reflection and Discussion

Review <u>The Map of Resentment</u> diagram (<u>Image 7 in the Appendix</u>), showing stages in development of resentment. Then, answer questions 1–4.

1. Examine the following list of situations that commonly produce frustration and check the ones apply to you.
    - o   Unresolved and buried anger
    - o   Unfulfilled needs and desires
    - o   Confusion about identity and/or role
    - o   Unaccepted losses
    - o   Lack of direction and meaningful goals
    - o   Unreasonable expectations and demands I place upon myself (such as perfection)
    - o   Unreasonable expectations and demands others have of me
    - o   Difficult circumstances which I cannot change

2. List any other causes of frustration that you have?


3. Which of the frustrations that you listed are within your boundary of control?


Read the following Scriptures; then answer question 4.

> "So humble yourselves under the mighty power of God, and at the right time he will lift you up in honor.

Give all your worries and cares to God, for he cares about you"

(1 Peter 5:6–7 NLT).

4. What can you do about the frustrations over which you have no control?


In his book *The Lies We Believe,* Dr. Chris Thurman talks about common lies people believe. The following list is some of the lies that could keep us trapped in resentment.

- "I Must Be Perfect"
- "I Must Have Everyone's Love And Approval"
- "I Can't Be Happy Unless Things Go My Way"
- "It's Somebody Else's Fault."
- "Life Should Be Fair"
- "You Can And Should Meet All My Needs"
- "It Is My Christian Duty To Meet The Needs Of Others"
- "A Good Christian Doesn't Feel Angry, Anxious Or Depressed"

5. Underline the lies that you believe; then, look up the following Scriptures and ask God to help you write statements of truth that you can use to replace the lies.


"I Must Be Perfect" (I John 1:8–10)

"I Must Have Everyone's Love and Approval" (Galatians 1:10)

"Life Should Be Fair" (John 16:33)

"I Can't Be Happy Unless Things Go My Way" (Proverbs 14:12)

"It's Somebody Else's Fault." (I John 1:5–10)

"You Can and Should Meet All My Needs" (Philippians 4:19)

"It Is My Christian Duty to Meet the Needs of Others" (Philippians 4:19)

"A Good Christian Doesn't Feel Angry, Anxious or Depressed" (Psalm 22)

6. Reread the description of indirectly lashing out (found in chapter 11) and describe any ways you lash out, either at others or yourself?

<u>Journal Opportunity:</u> Tell God about the discoveries that you made about yourself as you studied this chapter, share your frustrations with him, and write down what he says to you about them.

## 12. Embrace Truth and Discover Joy

**Key Concepts:**

- By accepting that life is full of frustration, we can focus on problem solving.
- Sharing our frustrations can provide us with new insights and give us hope for finding solutions.
- Reducing expectations will reduce our frustration load.
- Replacing grudge-bearing with gratitude is a doorway to joy.
- Joy empowers us and energizes us so that we can become more productive.
- When we take time to resolve our frustrations instead of ignoring them, they will not accumulate and we can focus on creative pursuits.

## Questions for Reflection and Discussion

Review the <u>Development of Joy</u> diagram (<u>Image 8 in the Appendix</u>) and answer the following questions.

> The psalmist says, "The righteous person faces many troubles, but the LORD comes to the rescue each time" (Psalm 34:19 NLT).

1. How does this statement compare with your expectation what life should be like?

2. If you can recall a time when the Lord rescued you from trouble, write something about it.

When we place requirements (expectations) on others, we make demands of them, try to control their behavior, and become frustrated when they fail to "measure up." Having desires for others (wanting and wishing that they would change instead of demanding that they do) reduces our frustration level because it frees us from the impossible task of controlling others.

3. Write down an expectation that you have that's making you feel frustrated, and ask God how you can change it to a desire.

Read the following Scripture and answer questions 4 and 5.

> "The Scriptures give us patience and encouragement so that we can have hope. May the patience and encouragement that come from God allow you to

> live in harmony with each other the way Christ Jesus wants"
>
> (Romans 15:4–5 NCV).

4. In what ways might receiving encouragement and patience from God alter expectations that you have of others?

5. Write down your unfulfilled desires, give them to God, and ask him to encourage you.

Read the following statement of Jesus' disciple, John. Then answer question 6.

> "Loving God means keeping his commandments, and his commandments are not burdensome" (1 John 5:3 NLT). Burdensome means troublesome. Something that troubles us makes us feel frustrated.

6. Do you agree or disagree with the statement that God's commandments are not troublesome (frustrating)? Explain your answer.

7. Talk to a supportive and non-judgmental friend (someone in your accountability group, if possible) about any grudge that you have toward God, and ask for help, so that you let go of your resentment.

8. If you are someone who hangs on to grudges, what do you think makes it hard for you to let go of them?

Journal Opportunity: If gratitude is it an effort for you, record gratitude statements in a journal for ten days. At the end of that time, note any changes in your gratitude level, and share your statements with a friend.

# 13. Admit to Stubborn Revenge

## Key Concepts:

- Partiality exists everywhere; all of us experience unjust treatment of one kind or another.
- It's when others either ignore or break the rules we live by, that we believe we are being treated unjustly, feel offended, and complain.
- Demanding justice is our natural reaction to injustice.
- Sometimes (even as Christians), we blame God for the injuries we receive; we believe that if he truly loved us, he'd have protected us from injury.
- Because he didn't protect us in the way we expected him to, we feel offended toward God and distrust him; instead of relying on him to intervene on our behalf, and we take justice into our hands.
- "Getting even" with those who've injured (or offended) us seems to us the appropriate method of justice; however, to protect ourselves from further injury, getting even usually means that the injury we exact is greater than the one we received.
- In order for us to achieve what we believe will be effective revenge, we pretend to be at peace with our offender, while at the same time that we are planning an attack.

- Our retaliation, instead of protecting us, prompts our offender to make a counterattack.
- Violence, pain, and alienation escalate making justice impossible to obtain.

## Questions for Reflection and Discussion

Review the Map of Revenge diagram (Image 9 in the Appendix), showing stages in development of revenge; then, answer questions 1–3.

1. What are the stages of revenge that you most often get stuck in?

2. List four or five rules that you live by and expect other people to honor.

3. How do you usually react (what do you do, think, or say) to those who fail to live by the rules that you listed in question two?

Study the following Scripture verses on the topic of revenge, ask the Holy Spirit to show you how they apply to your life, and then answer questions 4 and 5.

> You're familiar with the old written law, 'Love your friend,' and its unwritten companion, 'Hate your enemy'. I'm challenging that. I'm telling you to love your enemies. Let them bring out the best in you, not the worst. When someone gives you a hard time, respond with the energies of prayer, for then you are working out of your true selves, your God-created selves. This is what God does. He gives his best—the sun to warm and the rain to nourish—to everyone,

regardless: the good and bad, the nice and nasty. If all you do is love the lovable, do you expect a bonus? Anybody can do that. If you simply say hello to those who greet you, do you expect a medal? Any run-of-the-mill sinner does that. In a word, what I'm saying is, *Grow up*. You're kingdom subjects. Now live like it. Live out your God-created identity. Live generously and graciously toward others, the way God lives toward you.
—Matthew 5:43–48 (MSG)

4. Why do you think Jesus calls us to give up these "natural" reactions to injury?


5. Think of someone who has offended you and describe what it would look like to "love" that person?


Read the following verse and answer question 6.

> "The kisses of an enemy *are* deceitful"
> (Proverbs 27:6 NKJV).

6. What does pretending to be kind to someone you dislike reveal about yourself?


> This was Paul's instruction to the church at Rome. "Dear friends, never take revenge. Leave that to the righteous anger of God. For the Scriptures say, 'I will take revenge; I will pay them back,' says the LORD"
> (Romans 12:19 NLT).

7. According to the above verse what does God have (and we lack) that makes it impossible for us, but possible for him, to be fair in getting revenge?

Journal Opportunity: Tell God why it's difficult for you to give up your natural reactions to injury. Tell him about any fears that you have and listen to what he tells you.

## 14. Prefer Mercy and Obtain Freedom

### Key Concepts:

- Being a Christian does not exempt us from suffering rejection, injury, and persecution.
- Extending mercy, by choosing to forgive those who have hurt is, not a natural, or easy, reaction.
- Recognizing that we, ourselves, need mercy and receiving that mercy and forgiveness from Jesus Christ usually make us more willing to extend mercy to others.
- Extending forgiveness does not mean that we belittle or deny our injury; it means that instead of demanding restitution, we bear the cost of that injury and trust in God's provision for us.
- God is the only one who can exact impartial justice.
- Desiring justice rather than demanding justice places us in a position of trusting God.
- Relinquishing our right to get even puts us in a position to receive God's intervention.
- Forgiveness is one-sided; we can choose to forgive our offenders even if they do not receive it.
- Reconciliation is two-sided; we can't achieve it on our own; yet, God instructs us to desire and pray for it.
- It's wise and appropriate to set boundaries that will protect us from repeated injury and abuse.

- Choosing to bless those who've injured us facilitates emotional and spiritual integrity.

## Questions for Reflection and Discussion

Review the "Development of Mercy" diagram (Image 10 in the Appendix) and questions 1–3.

1. Which stage(s) in the development of mercy are you strong in? Give specific examples.

2. Which stage(s) in the development of mercy are you weak in? Give specific examples.

3. Ask the Holy Spirit to show you the area(s) that he wants you to grow in. Write down what he shows you.

Read the steps of forgiveness (found in chapter 14 and, also, listed below), then answer questions 4 and 5.

- Recognize the injury.
- Identify the emotions involved.
- Express your hurt and anger.
- Set boundaries to protect yourself.
- Cancel the debt.
- Consider the possibility of reconciliation.

4. Write down the step(s) of forgiveness that are easiest for you to recognize and/or which you are doing.

5. Write down the step(s) of forgiveness that are harder for you to recognize and/or which you are not doing.

6. Ask God to show you whom you most need to show mercy.

We might think that a "hunger and thirst for justice" would eliminate mercy, but Jesus places them together. Read the following Scripture and answer question 7.

> "God blesses those who hunger and thirst for justice, for they will be satisfied. God blesses those who are merciful, for they will be shown mercy"
> (Matthew 5:6–7 NLT).

Journal Opportunity: Think of a situation in which you now feel (or have felt) offended. Use this as an opportunity to journal; ask God to show you what it would look like for you to desire justice and, at the same time, be merciful.

Read the following Scripture and answer questions 7 and 8.

> God was in Christ, making peace between the world and himself. In Christ, God did not hold the world guilty of its sins. And he gave us this message of peace. So we have been sent to speak for Christ. It is as if God is calling to you through us. We speak for Christ when we beg you to be at peace with God. Christ had no sin, but God made him become sin so that in Christ we could become right with God.
> —2 Corinthians 5:19–21 (NCV)

7. In which category would you place yourself?
   A) Needing to come back to God and be reconciled with him, or
   B) Needing to share God's message of reconciliation with others.

8. If you need help in taking one of the above steps, ask God to show you whom you could talk to in order to receive that help. Write down the name of that person.

Read the following Scripture and answer question 9.

> "They are blessed who show mercy to others, for God will show mercy to them"
>
> (Matthew 5:7 NCV).

9. What does God promise us when we choose mercy instead of revenge?

# Appendix

## Image 1: "Tree" Model of Emotion

"A healthy tree cannot bear bad fruit, nor can a diseased tree bear good fruit" (Matthew 7:18 English Standard Version).

| THE UNHEALTHY TREE | THE HEALTHY TREE |
| --- | --- |
| **FRUIT** = Attitudes and behavior of the sin nature (Galatians 5:19-21)<br>**LEAVES** = Desires generated by the sin nature (Colossians 3:5-8)<br>**LIMBS & BRANCHES** = Destructive thought patterns (Genesis 6:5)<br>**ROOTS** = A deceptive and diseased heart (Jeremiah 17:9; Mark 7:21-23) | **FRUIT** = Attitudes and behavior like those of Jesus (2 Corinthians 3:18)<br>**LEAVES** = Desires generated by the Holy Spirit (Galatians 5: 22, 23)<br>**LIMBS AND BRANCHES** = A healthy thought life (Philippians 4:8)<br>**ROOTS** = A heart of truth and love (Hebrews 10:16; 2 Corinthians 5:14) |
| **OTHER INFLUENCES**<br>**SOIL** = Unhealthy generational patterns (Book of Genesis)<br>**CLIMATE** = Lies from Satan and the world (1 John 2:16; Matthew 4: 1-11)<br>**TYPE of TREE** = Limits of genetic predisposition (Psalm 103:13-16) | **OTHER INFLUENCES**<br>**SOIL** = Scripture and the Holy Spirit (Psalm 1 and 1 John 2:27)<br>**CLIMATE** = Support from the body of Christ (Ephesians 4:15-16)<br>**TYPE of TREE** = A new creation in Christ (2 Corinthians 5:17) |

Tree Drawing used with permission of Corinne Kelly Avery

# Image 2: Bonded to a Diseased Root—the Sin Nature

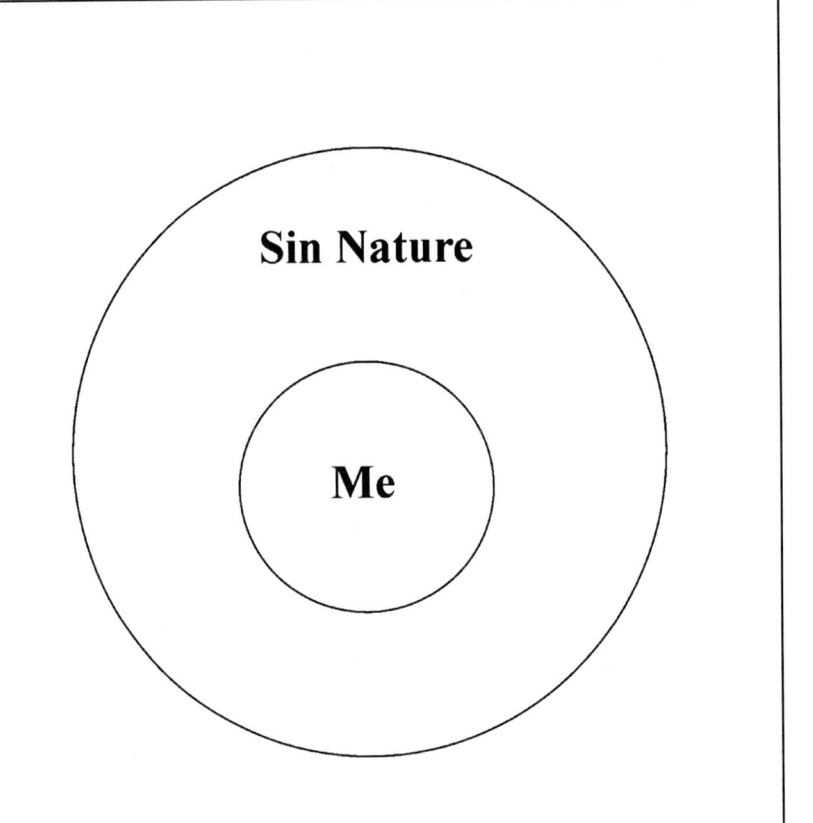

**Sin Nature**

**Me**

Like a chained handcuff attached to our will, the sin nature pulls us away from the "good" that we want to do and pushes us toward the "bad" that we try to avoid.

# Image 3: Set Free, by Christ, and Grafted into His Healthy Root

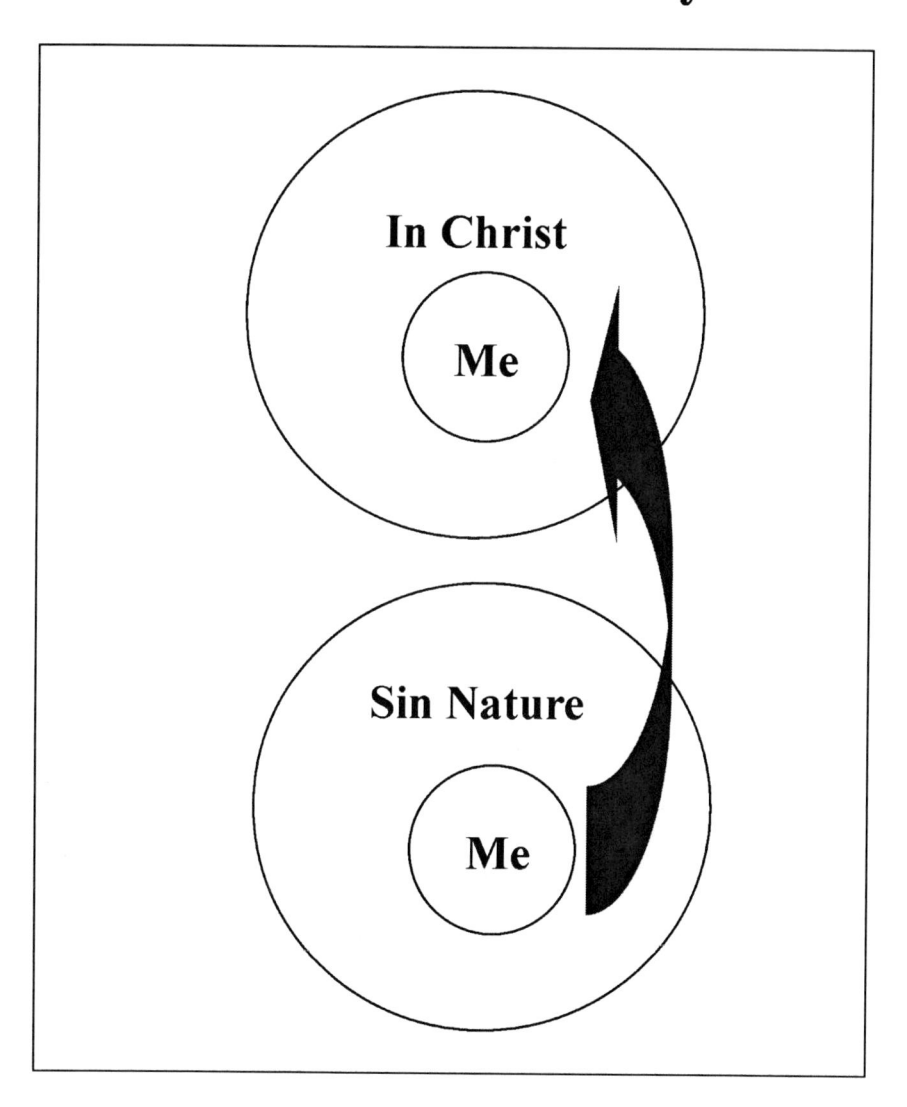

# Image 4: We Must Choose our Dance Partner—Jesus Christ or the Sin Nature

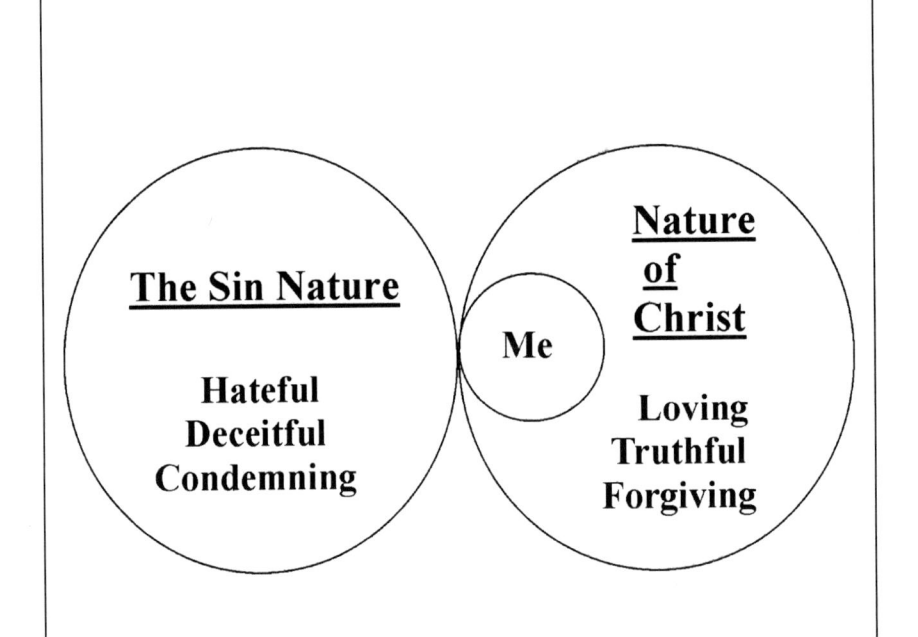

**The Sin Nature**

Hateful
Deceitful
Condemning

Me

**Nature of Christ**

Loving
Truthful
Forgiving

As we "dance" in a transparent relationship with Christ, his nature becomes a part of us. Grace and truth motivate our decisions and empower our behavioral changes.

# Image 5: Map of Destructive Anger (Addiction May Develop)

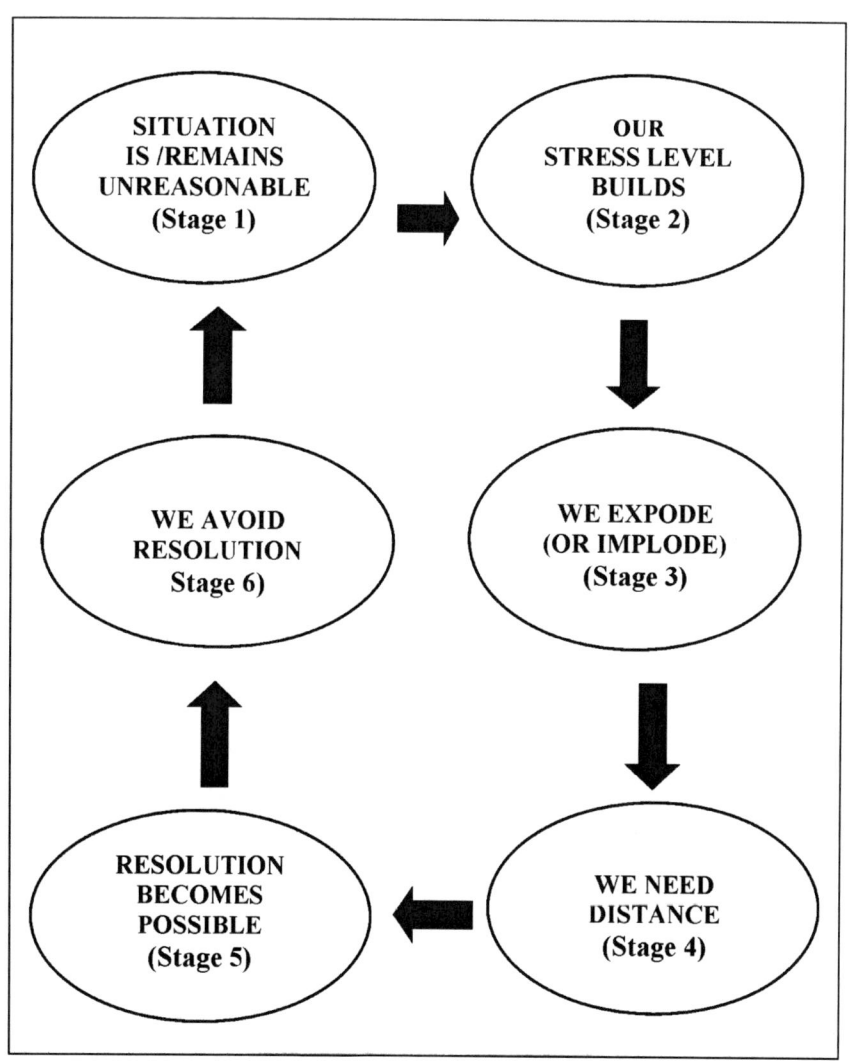

```
SITUATION IS/REMAINS UNREASONABLE (Stage 1) → OUR STRESS LEVEL BUILDS (Stage 2)
                                                        ↓
WE AVOID RESOLUTION (Stage 6)                  WE EXPODE (OR IMPLODE) (Stage 3)
       ↑                                                ↓
RESOLUTION BECOMES POSSIBLE (Stage 5) ← WE NEED DISTANCE (Stage 4)
```

Map Adapted from Peter Ladd

# Image 6: Development of Self-control (Constructive Anger)

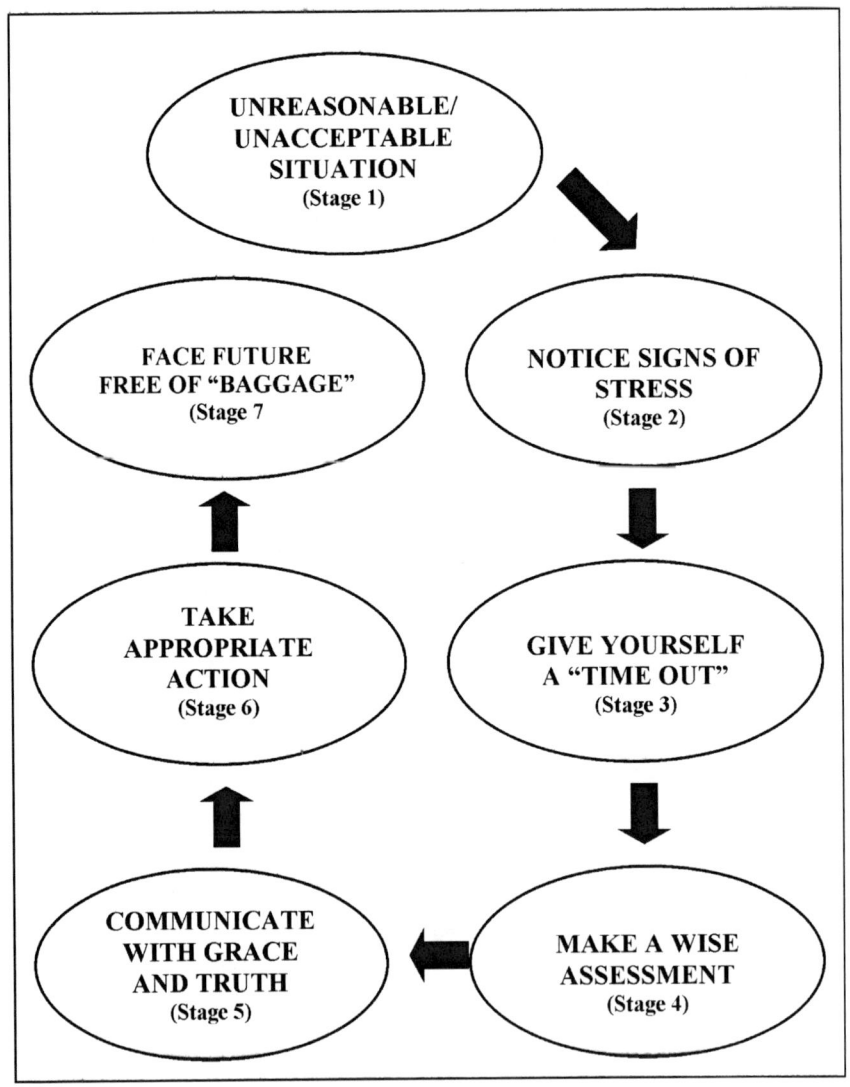

- UNREASONABLE/ UNACCEPTABLE SITUATION (Stage 1)
- NOTICE SIGNS OF STRESS (Stage 2)
- GIVE YOURSELF A "TIME OUT" (Stage 3)
- MAKE A WISE ASSESSMENT (Stage 4)
- COMMUNICATE WITH GRACE AND TRUTH (Stage 5)
- TAKE APPROPRIATE ACTION (Stage 6)
- FACE FUTURE FREE OF "BAGGAGE" (Stage 7)

**Map Adapted from Peter Ladd**

# Image 7: The Map of Resentment

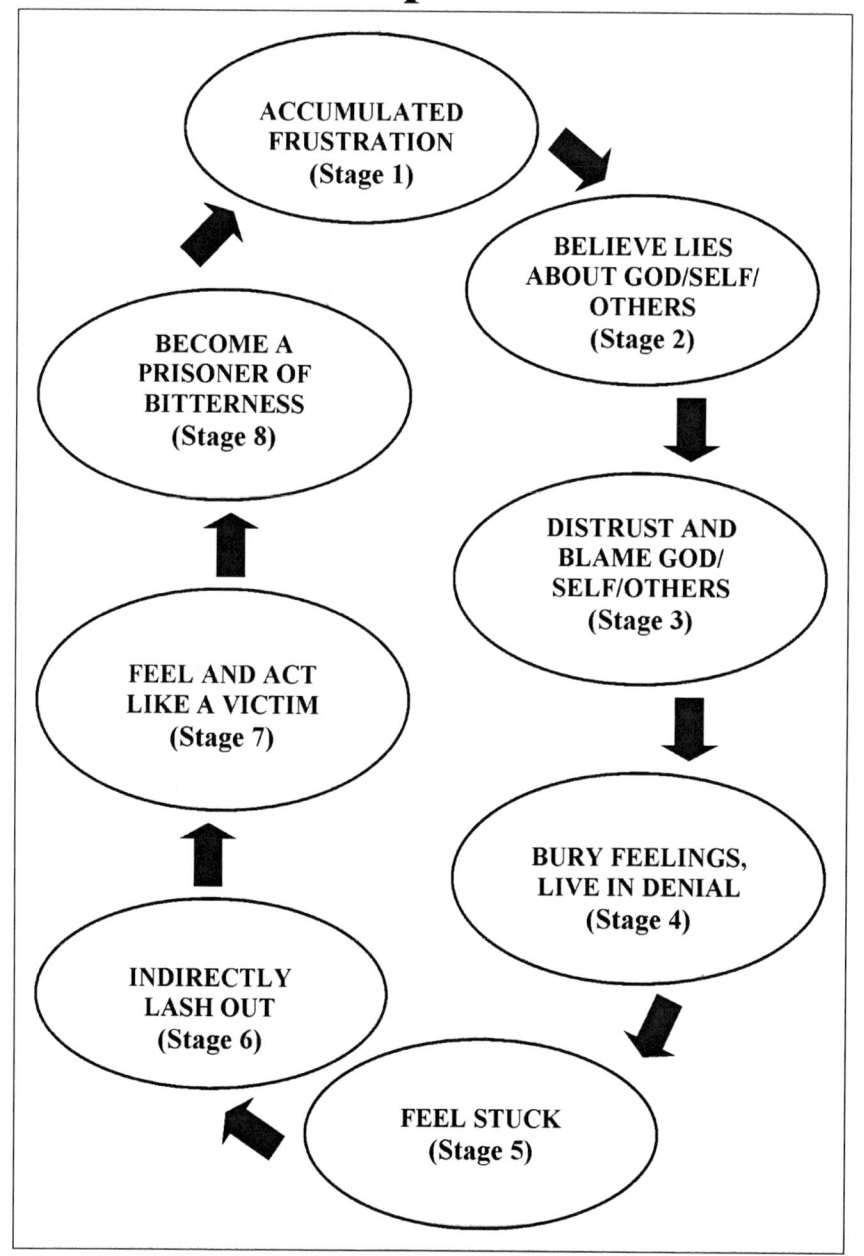

- ACCUMULATED FRUSTRATION (Stage 1)
- BELIEVE LIES ABOUT GOD/SELF/OTHERS (Stage 2)
- DISTRUST AND BLAME GOD/SELF/OTHERS (Stage 3)
- BURY FEELINGS, LIVE IN DENIAL (Stage 4)
- FEEL STUCK (Stage 5)
- INDIRECTLY LASH OUT (Stage 6)
- FEEL AND ACT LIKE A VICTIM (Stage 7)
- BECOME A PRISONER OF BITTERNESS (Stage 8)

**Map Adapted from Peter Ladd**

# Image 8: The Development of Joy

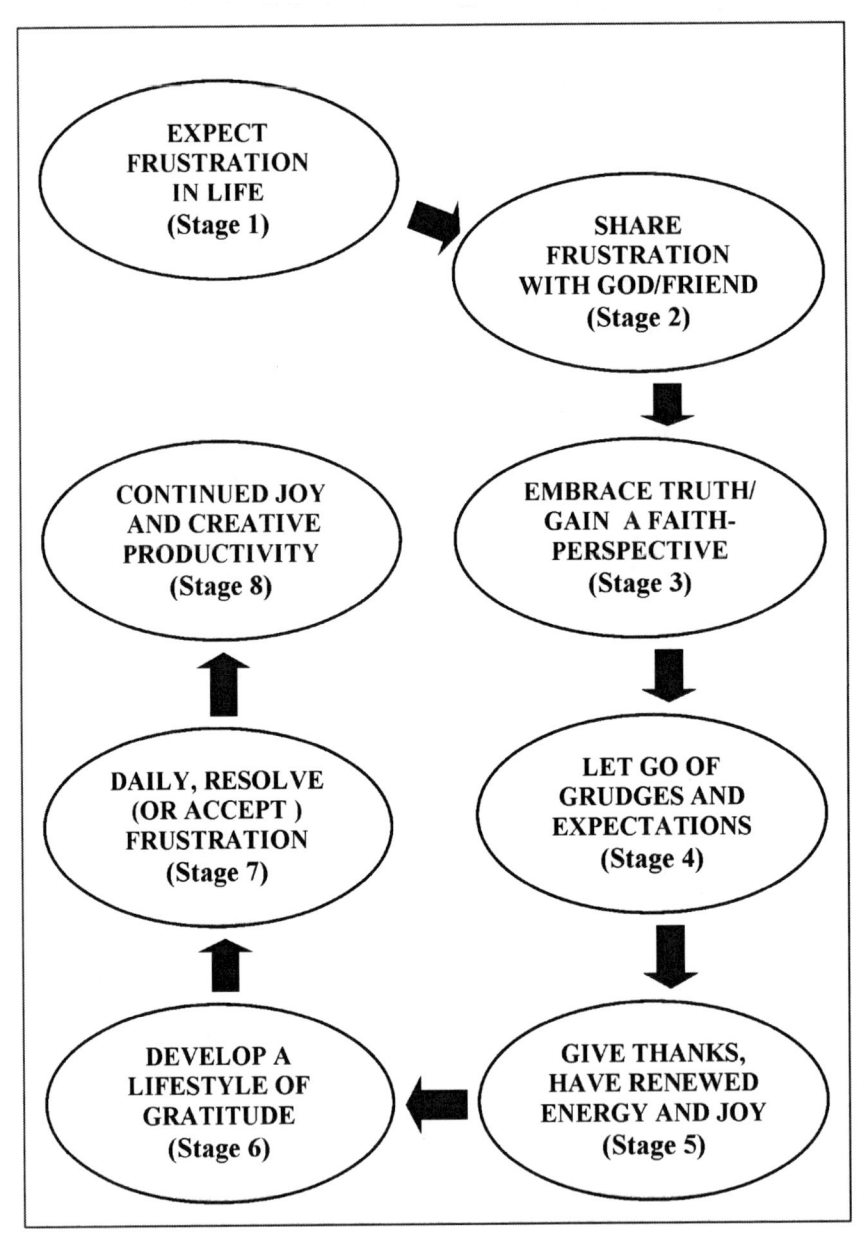

- **EXPECT FRUSTRATION IN LIFE** (Stage 1)
- **SHARE FRUSTRATION WITH GOD/FRIEND** (Stage 2)
- **EMBRACE TRUTH/ GAIN A FAITH-PERSPECTIVE** (Stage 3)
- **LET GO OF GRUDGES AND EXPECTATIONS** (Stage 4)
- **GIVE THANKS, HAVE RENEWED ENERGY AND JOY** (Stage 5)
- **DEVELOP A LIFESTYLE OF GRATITUDE** (Stage 6)
- **DAILY, RESOLVE (OR ACCEPT) FRUSTRATION** (Stage 7)
- **CONTINUED JOY AND CREATIVE PRODUCTIVITY** (Stage 8)

Map Adapted from Peter Ladd

# Image 9: The Map of Revenge

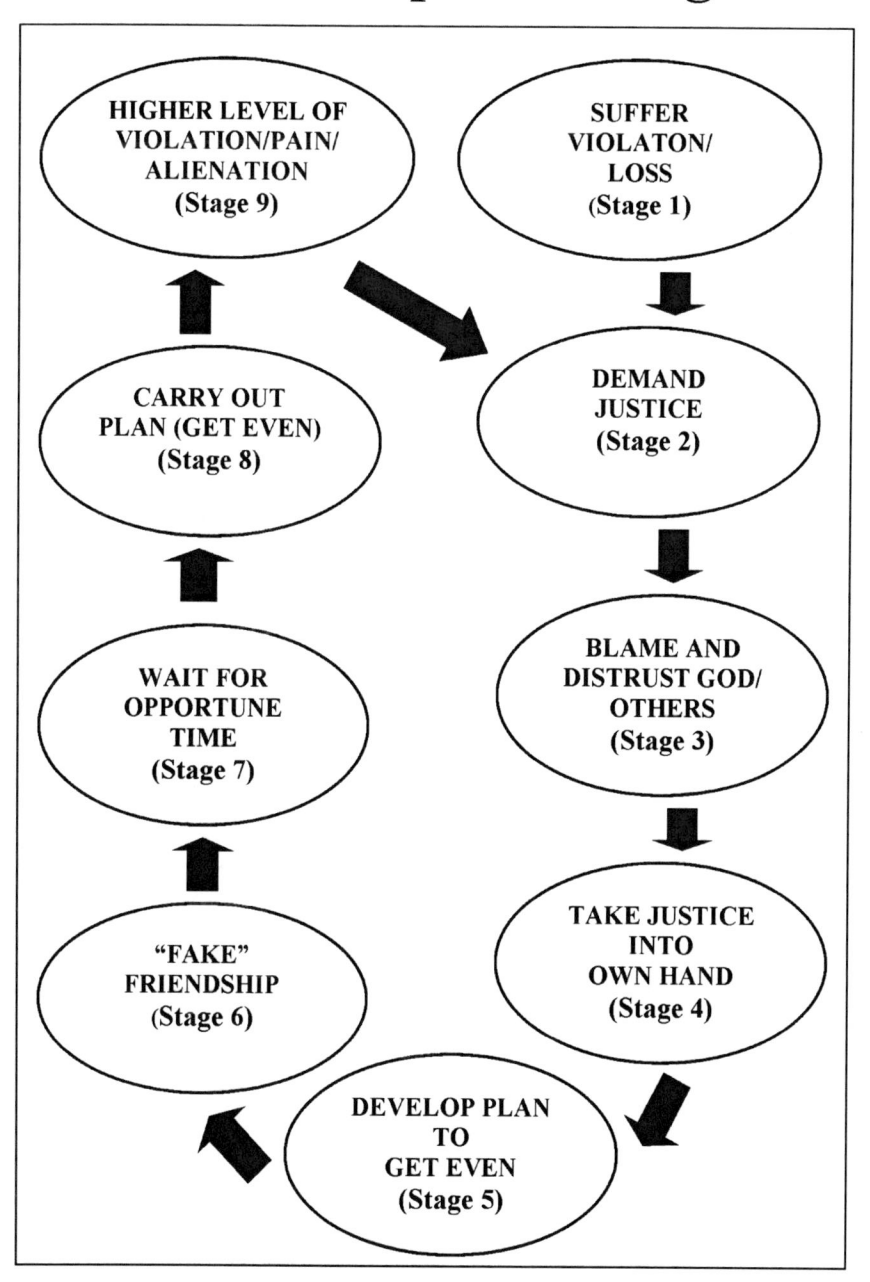

- HIGHER LEVEL OF VIOLATION/PAIN/ALIENATION (Stage 9)
- SUFFER VIOLATON/LOSS (Stage 1)
- CARRY OUT PLAN (GET EVEN) (Stage 8)
- DEMAND JUSTICE (Stage 2)
- WAIT FOR OPPORTUNE TIME (Stage 7)
- BLAME AND DISTRUST GOD/OTHERS (Stage 3)
- "FAKE" FRIENDSHIP (Stage 6)
- TAKE JUSTICE INTO OWN HAND (Stage 4)
- DEVELOP PLAN TO GET EVEN (Stage 5)

**Map Adapted from Peter Ladd**

# Image 10: Development of Mercy

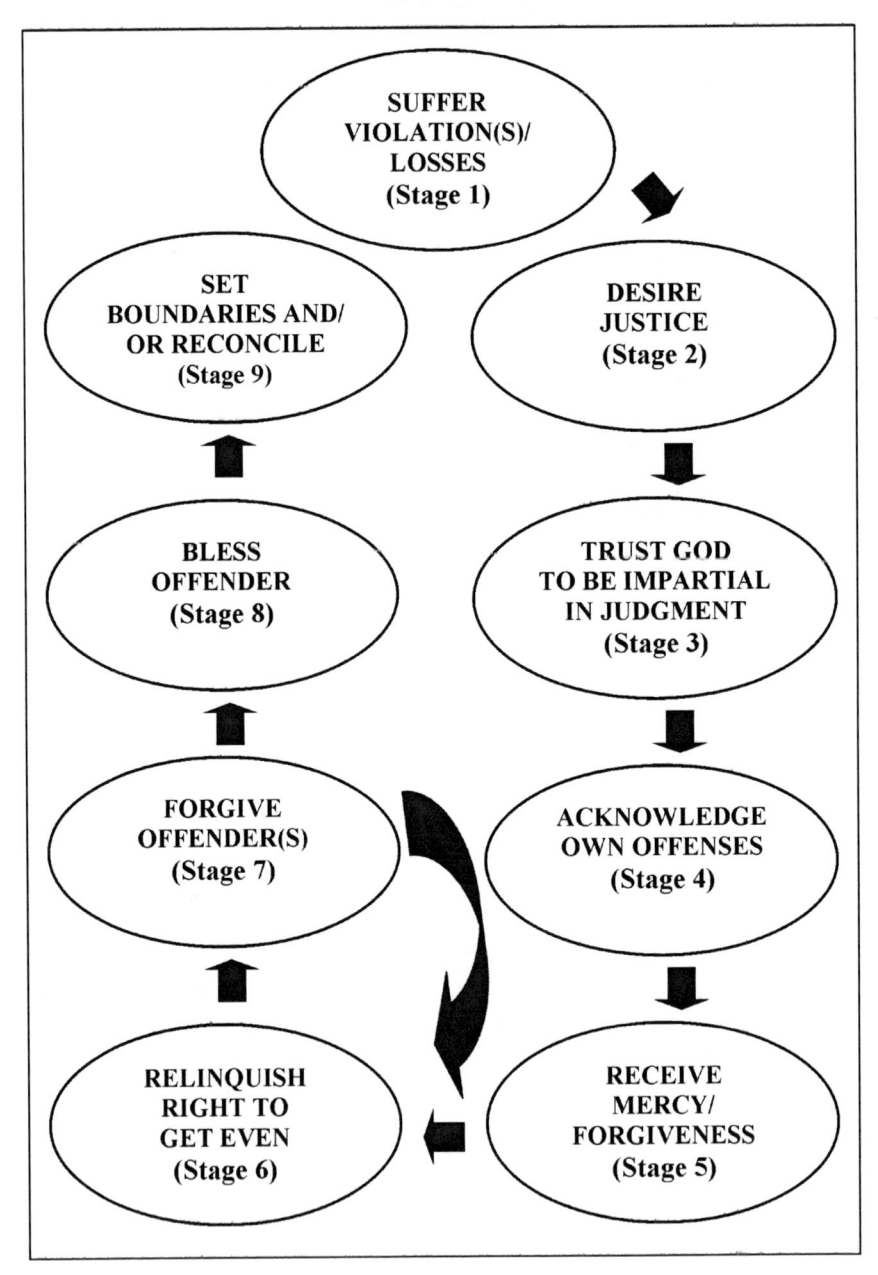

- SUFFER VIOLATION(S)/ LOSSES (Stage 1)
- DESIRE JUSTICE (Stage 2)
- TRUST GOD TO BE IMPARTIAL IN JUDGMENT (Stage 3)
- ACKNOWLEDGE OWN OFFENSES (Stage 4)
- RECEIVE MERCY/ FORGIVENESS (Stage 5)
- RELINQUISH RIGHT TO GET EVEN (Stage 6)
- FORGIVE OFFENDER(S) (Stage 7)
- BLESS OFFENDER (Stage 8)
- SET BOUNDARIES AND/ OR RECONCILE (Stage 9)

**Map Adapted from Peter Ladd**

# Notes

## 2. Aborted and Diseased "Fruit"

[1] http://biblehub.com/greek/5046.htm 9/10/2014

## 3. The "Tree" Model of Emotion

[1] Daniel Goldman, *Emotional Intelligence* (New York NY: Bantam Books, 1995), 4.
[2] Garrison Keillor, *Lake Woebegon Days* (New York, NY: Viking Penguin Inc., 1985), 8.
[3] Peter D. Ladd, *Emotional Addictions* (Lanham, MD: University Press of America, Inc., 2009), 4, 15,171, 195.
[4] Elaine N. Aron, The *Highly Sensitive Person* (New York, NY: Broadway Books, 1996), xii.

## 5. Bonded to a Diseased Root

[1] James Houston, *The Heart's Desire* (Batavia, Illinois: Lion Publishing, 1992), 52, 54.

## 8. Nutrients for Growth

[1] Richard J Foster, *Celebration of Discipline: The PATH to SPIRITUAL GROWTH* San Francisco: Harper1988. p. 7
[2] http://www.biblegateway.com/
[3] Henry Cloud and John Townsend, *Safe People* (Grand Rapids, MI: Zondervan, 1995), 41-60.

## 9. Identify Dysfunctional Anger

1. Neil Clark Warren, *Make Anger Your Ally* (Wheaton IL: Tyndale House Publishers 3rd edition 1990), p. 9-10.
2. Ibid.,113.
3. Hart, Archibald D., *Adrenaline and Stress* (Dallas, TX: Word Publishing, 1995) 32-33.

## 10. Choose Self-Control and Become Productive

1. James Houston, *The Heart's Desire* (Batavia, Illinois: Lion Publishing, 1992), 71.

## 11. Uncover Bitter Resentment

1. Neil Clark Warren, *Make Anger Your Ally* (Wheaton IL: Tyndale House Publishers 3rd edition, 1990), 171-172.
2. Chris Thurman, *The Lies We Believe* (Nashville, TN: Thomas Nelson, Inc., 1989), Table of Contents
3. John Piper, *Future Grace* (Sisters, OR: Multnomah Books, a part of the Questar publishing family, 1995), 94.

## 12. Embrace Truth and Discover Joy

1. Ann Morgan Voskamp, *One Thousand Gifts* (Grand Rapids, MI: Zondervan, 2010), 151-152.
2. Ibid., 176.
3. Richard Swenson, *In Search of Balance: Keys to a Stable Life* (Colorado Springs, CO: NavPress, 2010), 147-148.

## 13. Admit to Stubborn Revenge

1. Henry Cloud and John Townsend, *Boundaries* (Grand Rapids, MI: Zondervan, 1992), 31.
2. http://northcountrynow.com/north-country-this-week Nov 19- 25, 2014, 1-2.
3. West Virginia Encyclopedia http://www.wvencyclopedia.org/articles/314 March 25, 2013

## 14. Prefer Mercy and Obtain Freedom

[1] Kay Marshall Strom, *In the Name of Submission* (Portland OR: Multnomah Press, 1986), 56.
[2] Sandra Wilson, *Hurt People Hurt People* (Thomas Nelson Nashville 1993), 74-75.
[3] David Stoop and James Masteller, *Forgiving our Parents, Forgiving Ourselves* (Ann Arbor MI: Servant Publications, 1991), 269.
[4] Paul Hegstrom, *Angry Men and the Women Who Love Them* (Kansas City: Beacon Hill Press. Rev. ed. 2004), 115.

# About the Author

Jane Ault, in partnership with her husband-pastor, has mentored and counseled people from various economic, social, and cultural backgrounds for forty-three years—thirty-one in Potsdam, NY and twelve in Roanoke, VA. She received a M. Ed. in counseling and human development from Saint Lawrence University in Canton, NY. Part of her education included a preceptorship at St. Lawrence County Alcohol Services. Having integrated the truths of psychology with Scripture, she approaches the topic of emotional freedom from both a secular and a spiritual viewpoint.

Her personality, gifting, calling, long-term walk of faith in Jesus Christ, life experiences, and education have equipped Jane to speak about her topic with authority, knowledge, wisdom, and compassion. She's a poet, writer, teacher, and counselor.

A meditative, artistic woman of Scandinavian descent, Jane is by nature and gifting an introvert and a poet. Throughout the years, she's included poetry in her teaching and counseling practice. Her other artistic interests are photography, painting, card-making, piano, and song-writing. She's been married to her husband John for forty-eight years. They have two daughters and six grandchildren. John and Jane live on the shore of a small lake in northern New York.